R&D, Education,

and Productivity

R&D, Education, and Productivity

A Retrospective

ZVI GRILICHES

HARVARD UNIVERSITY PRESS

CAMBRIDGE, MASSACHUSETTS

LONDON, ENGLAND

2000

Library of Congress Cataloging-in-Publication Data

Griliches, Zvi, 1930–
R&D, education, and productivity : a retrospective / Zvi Griliches.
p. cm.
Includes bibliographical references and index.
ISBN 0-674-00343-8 (alk. paper)
1. Research, Industrial—Economic aspects.
2. Industrial productivity.
I. Title: R&D, education, and productivity.
II. Title: R and D, education, and productivity.
III. Title.
HC79.R4 G743 2001
338′.06—dc21
00-044881

To my wife

CONTENTS

ACKNOWLEDGMENTS

I am grateful to the editorial group that Mike Rothschild assembled, including Mark Schankerman, Timothy Taylor, Bob Gordon, and Mike himself, for helping me finish this book during my illness. Mark bore the brunt of the revisions of all the major chapters. I thank many close friends for their comments on earlier versions of the book, especially Tor Jakob Klette and Bob Gordon. I also thank Daehwan Kim, who performed the statistical analyses. I am greatly indebted to the yeoman's work of my secretary, Jane Trahan, who typed and retyped and assembled various versions of these chapters again and again. Without her it would have taken months longer to prepare the manuscript.

I thank the National Science Foundation for its lifetime support of my work. I also thank the Paul M. Warburg fund at Harvard University for financial support.

I am most grateful to my wife, Diane, who stood by me throughout the history of this work and especially during my recent illness.

Zvi Griliches
Cambridge, Massachusetts
October 1999

R&D, Education,

and Productivity

Introduction

This volume is a revision of the Simon Kuznets Memorial Lectures given at Yale University on October 30–31, 1997. They and this book examine from a personal point of view a major theme of my work since I began studying economics seriously in the mid-fifties: technical change and productivity growth. Chapter 1 (which appeared in a different form in the *Journal of Economic Literature*) recounts the discovery of the "residual" from the earliest discussions in the 1930s of ratios of output over input to Robert Solow's elegant (1957) reformulation, which only made the stylized facts starker and more troublesome. The lion's share of the observed growth in output was attributed to "technical change" or, more correctly, to the "residual."

My approach to this problem developed when I was a graduate student and a young faculty member at the University of Chicago in the mid-fifties. Theodore Schultz challenged me to look at technical change from the perspective of the effects of research and returns to scale in agriculture using the (then distinctive) empirical tradition of agricultural economics. Another important influence was an approach to econometrics that I absorbed largely from Trygve Haavelmo and Hans Theil. Haavelmo emphasized the importance of asking the right question and being sensitive to the possibility that the data are moved by forces other than those included in the model being considered at the moment. I like to think that this skeptical spirit is evident throughout this book.

In Theil's approach to specification analysis I found a paradigm for analyzing productivity and technical change. From this point of view, the spectacle of economic models yielding large residuals is rather unsatisfactory, even when the issue is fudged by renaming the residuals "technical change" and then claiming credit for their "measurement." A concern with specification analysis led naturally to a series of questions about the model used to compute such residuals and also about the ingredients—the data—used in the model's implementation. This led me to a research program that focused on the various components of such computations and alternatives to them. Chapter 2 uses this framework.

One of my approaches to explaining the "residual" was to adjust productivity measures for the changing quality of the labor force, especially its level of schooling. Both Edward F. Denison (1962 and 1964a) and I developed this idea at about the same time. My work was an empirical economist's response to the ideas of human capital that Theodore Schultz, Jacob Mincer, and Gary Becker were developing at that time at the University of Chicago. My labor quality adjustments used observed earnings differences by level of schooling to measure the relative quality of different workers. Such computations assume (1) that differences in earnings correspond to differences in contributions (marginal products) to national and sectoral output; and (2) that these differences are in fact due to schooling and not to other factors such as native ability or family background that happen to be correlated with schooling. These assumptions are obviously controversial. I was uneasy with "adjustments" for which there was no direct evidence. This discomfort was the motivation for a research program that investigated empirically the validity of such estimates of the contribution of education to productivity and economic growth. Chapter 3 reports the current status of this program; my view is that the original assumptions hold up pretty well.

I began my research into productivity in agricultural economics. My teacher Theodore Schultz actually attributed *all* of productivity growth in agriculture to public investments in agricultural research (Schultz 1953). There was at that time almost no quantitative evidence for the view that research and development affected productivity. It was my belief (and presumption) that one could use the then newly available econometric techniques to examine how productivity is produced. If one is to treat technical change as endogenous, as something that is being "produced" by the economic system and the actors in it, and not like some "manna from heaven," then one needs to look for its sources, for the activities that cause it, directly or indirectly. This point of view motivated my dissertation research on hybrid corn (Griliches 1957), as well as the research program that I, my students, and others have pursued since then. Chapter 4 (a revised version of Chapter 12 of *R&D and Productivity: The Econometric Evidence*, 1998) is the most technical chapter of this book. It describes the current status of this research program, its most important results, and the open questions—of which there are many.

Productivity increases are not inexorable and exponential. The United States and most of the rest of the world experienced a productivity slowdown in the 1970s from which we may now be recovering. (When exactly the productivity slowdown began is still being debated, but no one argues about whether it occurred.) An account of productivity increases ought to explain, or at least be consistent with, the productivity slowdowns. This question is examined in Chapter 5. In my brief concluding Chapter 6, I offer a few reminders that sometimes get lost in the rush toward modeling, as a guide both for those who use productivity numbers and for those who will carry forward the work in this exciting area into the future.

This book is a personal survey. I have not attempted to be either comprehensive or completely up to date. I have tried to convey my own view of what I regard as some of the most important and exciting areas in economics. The most vital theme is that one makes progress in economics by focusing on important questions. It is vital to use and develop new tools; this, after all, is how economists learn more. But one should never forget the question. A classic joke about economists tells the story of the economist who lost his car keys somewhere on a dark street. He

looks for the keys not where he lost them but under the street lamp, because that is where the light is. I would respond that the creative economist finds a flashlight, or uses the car's mirror to reflect the light, or if
necessary gets down on his hands and knees and grubs in the dark to
look for the keys where he thinks they are.

1

The Discovery of the Residual

The first use of the term "residual," or residual factor, in a discussion of productivity seems to have been made by H. W. Arndt in a paper that was written around 1961, although not published until 1964. The term first came into popular use in 1964, as the title of an Organization for Economic and Commercial Development (OECD) monograph, *The Residual Factor and Economic Growth* (Vaizey et al. 1964). Referring to the analysis of productivity in terms of the "residual" has become standard in the lexicon of economists. The term is especially apt for several reasons. It describes how productivity analysis was often done, especially in the 1940s and 1950s—ascribing any leftover or residual growth in measured output growth that cannot be "explained" by growth in measured inputs to changes in productivity. It serves as a reminder of a common finding of research on productivity—that the unexplained, residual element has been substantial in many studies and for many time periods. Finally, it conveys the main challenge of productivity research, which is to seek an economic explanation for this residual and how it has changed over time.

The modern study of productivity had been making dramatic steps forward for several decades before the "residual" term gained prominence. The concept of total productivity and the notion that labor is not the only factor of production, and that other factors such as capital and land should also be taken into account in a calculation or a measure of its productivity, were discussed repeatedly in the literature of the 1930s. Two major strands of research came together, ultimately, in what was to become total factor productivity measurement and growth "accounting." The first developed out of the national income measurement tradition, based largely on the work of the National Bureau of Economic Research (NBER) and what was later to become the Bureau of Economic Analysis (BEA) in the U.S. Department of Commerce.[1] The second was influenced by Paul Douglas's work on production functions. His work had been largely cross-sectional, but as time series data became available it was an obvious generalization to add trendlike terms to the function and allow it to shift over time. This research tradition had a more econometric background and, at least in the early years, did not pay much attention to the consistency of the main empirical finding (increasing returns to scale) with the underlying assumptions embedded in the construction of the national income accounts. This approach found a fertile soil in agricultural economics, spurred by the presence and teaching of Gerhard Tintner at Iowa State University (Tintner 1943) and the later work of Earl Heady (see Heady and Dillon 1961, chap. 1, for an early review of this literature). The two traditions came together in the work of Solow (1957), in some of my own early papers (Griliches 1960a and 1963a), and especially in Jorgenson and Griliches (1967). But the two traditions have also kept drifting apart.

Once one started thinking about "real" national income and worrying how to deflate it, it was a relatively short step to the idea that the two different sides of these accounts (product receipts and factor payments) could be deflated separately, with their own specific deflators, yielding measures of real product and real input and an associated measure of economic efficiency. The idea of deriving a productivity measure as a residual based on calculations of real output and real input was already in the air in the 1930s. In one early example, Simon Kuznets (1930, p. 14) used the "cost of capital and labor per pound of cotton yarn," the inverse of what would later become a total factor productivity index (if the cost is computed in constant prices), based on numbers taken from Ellison (1886), as a "[reflection of] the economic effects of technical improvement" and, a few sentences later, as a measure of "the effect of technical progress." More thorough research might unearth even earlier references. However, the first systematic example of what might be called an output-over-input index that I can find appears in Copeland (1937, p. 31):

> Income derived from an area may be deflated to show changes in the physical volume of services of labor and wealth employed by the economic system . . . [and] the deflated distributive shares may be compared with the deflated consumed and saved income to show changes in the efficiency of operation of the economic system.

A year later the idea was much more fleshed out by Copeland and Martin (1938, p. 112), who said:

> Construct an index of the physical volume of wealth used in production each year and weight it by the total property income in the period selected for the determination of weights. This weighted plant-hour series might then be added to a correspondingly weighted man-hour series to measure physical input for the economic system . . . [A] divergence is likely to appear between the movements of a series representing the physical volume of output (and input), and . . . this divergence is a rough measure of changes in the efficiency of our economic system.

In commenting on this paper, Milton Friedman, in one of his earliest appearances on the scene, interpreted the authors as saying "that a comparison of the two types of indices (output and input) provides a basis for estimating the degree of technical change" (1938, p. 126), and raised a number of doubts about whether it is feasible to construct reliable indexes of the various required components. After discussing the substitution bias that is implicit in any fixed-weight index construction, he went on to say (1938, pp. 126–127):

Add to this (the substitution bias) the necessity of assuming "constant tastes," if the comparison is to be meaningful, and the difficulty of obtaining an adequate measure of the quantity of capital . . . as well as the lesser difficulties with the other factors of production, and the possibility of actually employing the procedure suggested by . . . Copeland and Martin seems exceedingly small. The derivation of a measure of "real input" that would provide an adequate basis for measuring changes in economic efficiency is even more complicated and difficult than the measurement of "real output'''; for the former involves the latter and other difficulties as well . . . We can . . . ask the question—to what extent is the change in output over some specified period a result of a change in the quantity of available resources, . . . [or] the way these resources are employed. (This separation is to a considerable extent artificial: technological change affects not only the way in which resources are employed but also the quantity and the character of the resources themselves.) In order to answer this question it would be necessary to determine the volume of "real output" that *would* have been produced had the techniques remained unchanged. A comparison of this series with the actual "real output" then provides a measure of the change in efficiency.

Copeland and Martin responded (1938, p. 134):

The measurement difficulties about which Mr. Friedman is concerned do not seem to have deterred others to the same extent. Dr. Kuznets has already provided measures of deflated national income in an output sense. Dr. Kuznets' measures of capital formation necessarily involve measurements of the quantities of all kinds of capital . . . Moreover . . . estimates of total man-years of employment have been developed. Thus . . . the two main elements for measurements of changes in social input (except . . . for non-reproducible wealth . . .) are admittedly at hand.

It must . . . be conceded that (such) measurements . . . are certain to be rough under present conditions. However, those who insist on a high degree of precision had best choose some field of activity other than estimating national wealth and income.

Remember, this discussion was taking place in 1937!

A little bit later, in 1940, Hicks considered a similar approach to "efficiency" measurement and added an explicit discussion of index number biases, noting that the problem "is much worse when we allow for increasing returns and imperfect competition" (p. 121). He also asked whether taxes should be included in the weights (his answers were yes for output indexes, no for input).

THE FIRST CALCULATIONS

Actual measurement of "productivity," "efficiency," or "technical change" (no sharp distinction was drawn at that time) was initiated by several people, working independently but subject to the same intellectual milieu. Whether they measured it as a shifter of the production function (Tinbergen 1942; Tintner 1944; Johnson 1950; Solow 1957) or as an output-over-total-input index (Stigler 1947; Barton and Cooper 1948; Schmookler 1952; Fabricant 1954; Ruttan 1954 and 1956; Kendrick 1955 and 1956; Abramovitz 1956), they did not claim any particular originality for it. They were making illuminating calculations for an idea that was obviously already there.

Credit for the earliest explicit calculation belongs clearly to Tinbergen (1942), published in German.[2] Douglas's production function work had already been criticized earlier for not allowing for some kind of trend factor in his estimating equation, especially by Mendershausen (1938), a criticism that Tinbergen endorsed in his *Econometrie* textbook, published in Dutch in 1941.[3] In the 1942 paper, Tinbergen was constructing a long-term growth model and needed an estimate of the trend in aggregate productivity growth. For this purpose he generalized the Cobb-Douglas production function by adding an exponential trend to it, intended to represent various "technical developments," and computed the average value of this trend component, calling it a measure of "efficiency," for four countries: Germany, Great Britain, France, and the United States, using the formula $t = y - 2/3n - 1/3k$, where y, n, and k are the average growth rates of output, labor, and capital respectively, and the weights, which represent output elasticities estimated from an aggregate production function, are taken explicitly from Douglas. Today economists would call this "calibration" rather than "estimation." Note how close this is to Solow (1957), who would let these weights change, shifting the index number formula from a fixed-weight geometric to an approximate Divisia form. Nobody seems to have been aware of Tinbergen's paper in the United States until much later. Valvanis-Vail (1955) mentioned Tinbergen but, it is obvious from the context, not this paper. Following a suggestion attributed to Arnold Harberger, he used average factor shares to compute a Cobb-Douglas–type total input index and a residual that he then used to estimate the trend coefficient for an aggregate production function, yielding an estimate of 0.75 percent per year for the 1869–1953 period. This was essentially equivalent to what Tinbergen did, but with weights based on income shares rather than estimated production function coefficients. Solow did reference Valvanis-Vail, but obviously neither of them was aware of Tinbergen (1942) at that point.

The developments in the United States originated primarily at the NBER, where a program of constructing national income and "real" output series under the leadership of Simon Kuznets was expanded also to include capital series for major sectors of the economy, with contributions by Creamer, Fabricant, Goldsmith, Tostlebe, and others. It seemed reasonably obvious to try and use such capital numbers in a more general productivity calculation.[4] At approximately the same time, parallel work on the measurement of output and input in agriculture was proceeding at the Bureau of Agricultural Economics (BAE) of the U.S. Department of Agriculture (USDA).

The first such published U.S. calculation appeared in 1947 in George Stigler's book *Trends in Output and Employment*, where, after working pretty hard on the output and employment data, he presented (on p. 49), off-handedly, what looks like a "back of the envelope" calculation of efficiency, which he stated "was usually defined as Output/(Input of Labor + Input of Other Resources)," for twelve manufacturing industries. In 1952, Jacob Schmookler, who had been Kuznets's student at the University of Pennsylvania, published a detailed article titled "Changing Efficiency of the American Economy," in which he constructed an output-over-total-input index with the intent "to describe the pattern and magnitude of technical change."[5]

At the same time that the NBER was assembling data for the U.S. economy as a whole and for several of its major sectors, a parallel measurement effort was proceeding at the BEA, directed at the measurement of farm output and efficiency. In 1948, Barton and Cooper published a fully articulated and detailed output-per-unit-of-input index for U.S. agriculture. Without computing such an index explicitly, Johnson (1950) used their data to estimate the magnitude of the shifts in the aggregate agricultural production function in different periods, based on weights from estimated production functions, both linear and linear in the logarithms of the variables.[6] Schultz (1953) used the Barton and Cooper index to compute the return to public investments in agricultural research. Ruttan (1954), as part of his dissertation at the University of Chicago, constructed linear and geometric output-over-input indexes for meat-packing plants, interpreting these indexes as approximations to shifts in the underlying production function. He used base and end period weights to bound them, and included a reasonably complete discussion of the potential biases in such a construction. An extension of this work to the measurement of "The Contribution of Technological Progress to Farm Output" was published in Ruttan (1956).

THE SYNTHESIZERS AND THE SURPRISE
AT THE SIZE OF THE RESIDUAL

The "raw materials" assembled by the NBER were used repeatedly in subsequent studies, and in 1953 Kendrick was asked to systematize and develop this line of measurement more explicitly. Calculations based on his preliminary work were made by Fabricant in 1954, who may have been the first to emphasize loudly that most of the growth in output per unit of input had not been explained and hence "it follows that the major source of our economic advance has been a vastly improved efficiency" (p. 8). In 1956, a much more detailed analysis of basically the same data was published by Abramovitz, who identified productivity with his computed index of "output per unit of utilized resources" and observed that "the lopsided importance which it appears to give to productivity increase" (in accounting for the growth in output per man-hour) "should be . . . sobering, if not discouraging, to students of economic growth." He went on to label the resulting index "a measure of our ignorance." Kendrick's own similar results had already been reported in the 1955 NBER Annual Report (Kendrick 1955, pp. 44–47), but his magnum opus was not published until 1961 (Kendrick 1961), and in the end he was overshadowed and did not get enough credit, in my opinion, either for providing the data to his "interpreters" or for the detailed data construction effort behind it. Some of these computations, and the parallel ones made for agriculture, are summarized in Table 1.1.

Against this historical background the 1957 paper by Solow may appear to be less original than it really was. Neither the question, the data, nor the conclusion was new. Nor did using a geometric input index with shifting weights affect the results all that much. What was new and opportune in Solow's paper, the "new wrinkle" (p. 312), was the explicit integration of economic theory into such a calculation. Solow brought together the national income accounting and production function approaches, thus uniting the subject analytically and providing an economic interpretation for the index number calculations. This paper showed that one need not assume stable production function coefficients to make such calculations. He provided an approximation formula for any constant returns production function and, by implication, also an interpretation of the earlier work that did not use this formula. This clarified the meaning of what were heretofore relatively arcane index number calculations and brought the subject from the periphery of the field to the center. It also connected it, indirectly, to Solow's seminal paper on growth theory (1956), and more generally to growth theory and macroeconomics as they were to develop subsequently. This was a masterly achievement that had an immense influence on subsequent work in both macro and micro economics.

Table 1.1. Early estimates of the "residual" in U.S. growth (percentage of growth not accounted for by conventional inputs).

		TOTAL ECONOMY		AGRICULTURE		
SOURCE	PERIOD	IN OUTPUT	IN OUTPUT PER EMPLOYEE OR EMPLOYEE HOUR	SOURCE	PERIOD	IN OUTPUT
Tinbergen (1942)	1870–1914	27	100			
Stigler (1947), selected man- ufacturing industries	1904–1937	n.a.	median 89	Barton and Cooper (1948)	1910–45	57
Schmookler	1869–1938	37	n.a.	Johnson (1950)	1900–20	24
(1952), manuf.	1969–1928	31	88		1923–29	50
					1940–48	50
Fabricant (1954)	1870–1950	n.a.	92	Ruttan (1956)	1910–50	
					beg. wts.	88
					end wts.	71
Kendrick (1955), manuf.	1899–1948		87			
Abramovitz (1956)	1869–1878 to 1944–53	48	86			
Solow (1957)	1909–1949	52	88			

Note: n.a. = not available; beg. wts. = beginning period weights; end wts. = end of period weights.
Source: Griliches (1996, p. 1327).

All of the pioneers of this subject were quite clear about the tenu-ousness of their calculations and that it might be misleading to identify the results as "pure" measures of technical progress. Abramovitz wor-ried about possible measurement errors in his labor and capital series, especially the omission of intangible capital accumulation through edu-cation, nutrition, and R&D, and also about not allowing for increasing returns to scale. Kendrick (1956) also noted the omission of intangible capital, such as R&D, from his total input construction. Solow empha-sized that he used "the phrase 'technical change' for *any kind of shift* in the production function" (emphasis in the original). He commented on the absence of good measures of capital utilization, and he credited Schultz for "a heightened awareness that a lot of what appears as shifts in the production function must represent improvement in the quality of the labor input, and therefore a result of real capital formation of an important kind" (note 8 in Solow 1957). Schultz, as mentioned earlier, actually attributed such numbers to public R&D and used them to compute a rate of return to R&D, influencing my subsequent work on returns to hybrid corn research (Griliches 1958). Most writers echoed Abramovitz's conclusion that such calculations should be interpreted, primarily, as providing an "indication of where we need to concentrate our attention."

At this point the gauntlet had been thrown down: even though it had been named "efficiency," "technical change," or most accurately a "measure of our ignorance," much of observed economic growth remained unexplained. It was now the turn of the explainers.

2

The Search for Explanations

By the early 1960s, it was well established that it was difficult to explain the growth in national output over time simply in terms of the growth in inputs. Many studies had consistently found a large residual of output growth remaining, unaccounted for by the growth in inputs, which was interpreted as "technical change" in the broadest sense of that term. Total factor productivity, as the "residual" later came to be known, had risen very substantially over the past hundred years, though there had sometimes been sharp fluctuations (see Figure 2.1). The next step was to "explain" this residual somehow.[1]

TWO ALTERNATIVE STYLES OF RESEARCH

The first approach, which remains popular to this day, was to treat the computed residual as a dependent variable and bring in various explanatory variables in some kind of regression framework to explain it, "account" for it, or validate a particular interpretation. The second approach tried to "explain" the computed residual by focusing on adjustments to the measurement of the various input and output components, with some justification from economic theory, in order to arrive at an overall assessment. Griliches (1960a), Denison (1962), and Jorgenson and Griliches (1967) provide examples of the latter. My own earlier work, whose outline was first alluded to by Schultz in 1956 but emerged

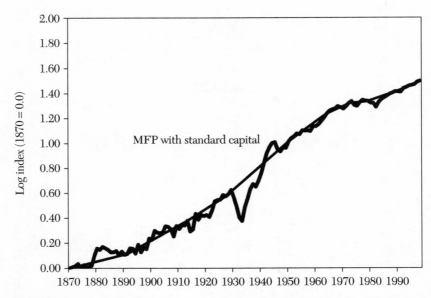

FIGURE 2.1   Multifactor productivity (MFP) in the nonfarm, nonhousing private economy, 1870–1998. (Source: Gordon 2000, fig. 3.)

in published form only later (in Griliches 1960a, 1963a,c, and 1964), bridges these two approaches, looking at separate pieces but using regression techniques to test and "validate" some of the suggested adjustments.

Denison's work (1962) was the most prominent of the first-generation attempts to explain the residual. His study was commissioned by the Committee on Economic Development, a business-funded think tank in Washington, D.C., to provide suggestions on how the rate of growth of the American economy could be improved. For this purpose he undertook a fresh analysis of the calculation of the "residual," tried to eliminate various measurement biases, and guessed at reasonable magnitudes for some of the unmeasured factors, such as economies of scale. At the end of the day he was left with a much smaller but still substantial residual, which he dubbed "advances in knowledge." The main conclusions of his work and the work of other first-generation explainers are summarized in Table 2.1. The "conventional residual" in that table re-

Table 2.1. Early "explanations" of the residual.

SOURCE AND MAJOR EXPLANATORY FACTORS	SECTOR	PERIOD	CONVENTIONAL RESIDUAL	ADJUSTED RESIDUAL	PERCENT UNEXPLAINED
Griliches (1960): capital measurement error, education	Agriculture	1948–58	2.16	1.60	74
Denison (1962): education and economies of scale	Total private economy	1929–57	2.01	0.59	29
Griliches (1963a): input measurement error, education, economies of scale	Agriculture	1940–60	1.96	−0.30	0
Griliches (1967): education and capital measurement errors	Manufacturing	1947–60	1.98	0.64	32
Griliches (1964): education, economies of scale, public R&D	Agriculture	1949–59	1.24	−0.02	0
Jorgenson-Griliches (1967): education, capital mismeasurement, and utilization	Total private economy	1945–65	1.60	0.10	5
Jorgenson-Griliches (1972): education and capital mismeasurement	Total private economy	1950–62	1.90	1.03	54

fers to the residual computed by looking at the measured outputs and inputs without adjustments for economies of scale, capacity utilization, human capital, R&D, measurement error, and so on. The "adjusted residual" contains an attempt to adjust for at least some of these factors.

My own interest in this subject was stimulated by listening to Schultz lecture and by reading his book *The Economic Organization of Agriculture* (1953). In that book he emphasized the importance of the contribution of technical change to output growth in agriculture, interpreted it largely as a product of the publicly supported R&D in the agricultural experiment stations, and noted that this type of technical change was not "manna from heaven" but required the investment of resources and was subject to economic influences and considerations. He elaborated further on this theme and on the importance of the changing quality of labor input in his 1956 paper, "Reflections on Agricultural Production, Output, and Supply." In commenting on an early draft of this paper I wrote:

> It will be useful if we can answer the following question: If we had all the resources in the world, no problems of errors in measurement, and unlimited computational facilities, what would we put in the "input" index? What would be the weights?
>
> Hunch: If we had an "ideal" input index, output over input would stay close to 1. By constructing such a theoretically ideal index and comparing it with the available "conventional" index, and observing wherein they differ, we may begin to understand what makes "observed" output over input tick.
>
> I think that it could be made more explicit how much this is . . . a problem of [the] changing "quality" of *all* inputs, not just labor . . . a tautological definition . . . such that output/input = 1, may prove useful for what is going on. One may allow this index to depart from one for "pure-pure" technological change, a larger output from *exactly the same* bundle of resources, e.g. the feeding of thousands on three loaves of bread!
>
> Unless we know what we want, we cannot interpret what we have.[2]

These ideas provided the impetus for my early work on agricultural data. Also, coming at it from a more econometric point of view, I was inclined to interpret the large "residual" as an indication of some kind of specification error. A good model of growth should fit better! What are the possible specification errors here?

THE MEASUREMENT PROBLEM: A MORE FORMAL STATEMENT

At this point it may be useful to sketch out a more explicit statement of the productivity measurement problem. The conventional measure of residual technical change, total factor productivity (TFP), in an industry can be written as

$$(2.1) \qquad \hat{t} = y - sc - (1 - s)n$$

where y, c, and n are percentage rates of growth in output, capital, and labor respectively; s is the share of capital in total factor payments; and the relevant notion of capital corresponds to an aggregate of actual machine hours weighted by their respective base period (equilibrium) rentals. Equation (2.1) simply says that the conventional measure of residual technical change is the growth in measured outputs minus the growth in measured inputs.[3] This procedure assumes that all the variables are measured correctly, that all the relevant variables are included, and that factor prices represent adequately the marginal productivity of the respective inputs. The last assumption is equivalent to the assumption of competitive equilibrium and constant returns to scale. To analyze t, the "unexplained" part of output growth, it is useful first to think in terms of a more general underlying production function:

$$(2.2) \qquad y^* - f = \alpha(c^* - f) + \beta(n^* - f) + \gamma z + t$$

$$(2.3) \qquad y = y^* + u$$

where the "true" production function is defined in terms of correctly measured outputs and inputs (the starred magnitudes) and at the technologically more relevant plant or firm level. Here f is the rate of growth in the number of plants (firms) in the industry, and the production function is thus defined implicitly at the average plant level. The parameters α and β are the true elasticities of output with respect to capital and labor, while γ is the elasticity of output with respect to the z's, the (rates of growth of) inputs that affect output but are not included in the standard accounting system. These could be services from the accumulated stock of past private research and development expenditures, services from the cumulated value of public (external) investments in research and extension in agriculture and other industries, or measurable disturbances such as weather or earthquakes. The measurement error in output is u. It differs from t in being more random and transitory while the forces behind t are thought to be more permanent and cumulative. The α, β, and γ coefficients need not be constants. If they are, we have the Cobb-Douglas case. The whole framework can be complicated and generalized by adding square and cross-product terms in rates of growth of the inputs as an approximation to any "flexible functional form," such as the constant elasticity of substitution (CES) or translog production function.

The framework in Equations (2.2) and (2.3) does two things. First, it adjusts for scale effects at the firm level by using f. It expresses both output and input growth relative to the growth in the number of plants. Another way of thinking about this adjustment is that growth is now being defined at the level of the average plant. This formulation highlights the distinction between possible increasing returns at the level of the micro unit (plant or firm) and those that arise at the industry or aggregate level, which reflect technological gains that are not captured fully by the micro unit. The second major adjustment is to recognize that this measure of output growth contains a "measurement" error, as shown in Equations (2.3). The measurement errors in capital and labor input are reflected in the distinction between n and n^*, and c and c^*, in Equations (2.1) and (2.2).

Define two more shorthand terms, $s^* = \alpha/(\alpha + \beta) = \alpha/(1 + h)$, where s^* is the "true" share of capital, and $h = \alpha + \beta - 1$ is a measure of economies of scale with respect to the conventional inputs c and n. With a little algebra, we can derive the following expression for the total "error" in our usual measures of total factor productivity growth:[4]

$$(2.4) \quad \hat{t} - t = s(c^* - c) + (1 - s)(n^* - n) + (s^* - s)(c^* - n^*)$$
$$+ h[s^*c^* + (1 - s^*)n^* - f] + \gamma z + u$$

The various terms in this formula can be interpreted as follows: The first term is the effect of the rate of growth in the measurement error of conventional capital measures on the estimated "residual." The second term reflects errors in the measurement and definition of labor input. The third term reflects errors in assessing the relative contribution of labor and capital to output growth. It would be zero if factor shares were in fact proportional to their respective production function elasticities or if all inputs were growing at the same rate (then the relative weights do not matter).[5] The fourth term is the economies of scale term. It would be zero if there were no underlying economies of scale in production ($h = 0$) or if the rate of growth in the number of new micro units (firms or plants) just equaled the growth in total (weighted) input, so that the average size of the micro unit is constant. The fifth term (γz) reflects the contribution of left-out inputs (private or public), while the sixth term (u) represents the various remaining errors in the measurement of output. It is important to emphasize that t itself is not fully exogenous either. It is a function of the *diffusion* of the new, best-practice technology, and the availability of such a technology is itself the partial product of science, engineering, and learning by doing. Moreover, in empirical implementations, the adjustments to measured inputs and outputs which we use to approximate Equation (2.2) are themselves likely to be imperfect.

This decomposition of the "error" in conventional measures of total factor productivity carries over to any level of aggregation. The list of issues identified by the decomposition provides a unifying framework for what at times appear to be rather disparate strands of work and has dominated my own range of research activities.

EMPIRICAL EFFORTS TO CREATE
IMPROVED MEASURES OF INPUTS

Both Denison and I gave major attention to education, as the source of improvements in the quality of the labor force, and to economies of scale. However, I focused more on measurement errors in capital, especially its price deflators, which led me to work on the measurement of quality change and hedonic prices at about the same time (Griliches

1961), and on the contribution of public investments in agricultural research, and on validating such adjustments (explanations) econometrically. By the time I included all of these factors, and some others, in a complete accounting, I not only succeeded in "explaining" the whole residual but actually "overexplained" it! (Griliches 1963a and 1964). The main conclusions of this work still seem to me right today: the major proximate sources of measured productivity growth in a sector are improvements in the quality of its labor force, improvements in the quality of inputs purchased from other industries, locally increasing returns to scale (at the enterprise level), and the contribution of public and private R&D in the form of better production and organizational techniques.

The Griliches and Jorgenson (1966) and Jorgenson and Griliches (1967) papers represented, in a sense, both the culmination and the end of this particular line of research. They claimed that a "correct" index number framework and the "right" measurement of inputs would largely eliminate the role of the residual and account for most of the observed growth in output. They brought together Jorgenson's earlier work on the cost of capital and index number theory with my own earlier work on quality change, biases in investment goods deflators, and the contribution of education to productivity growth. Jorgenson had shown how to derive the conceptually appropriate formula for the (opportunity) cost of capital from the economic theory of capital accumulation, and this in turn implied the right way of designing weights for the various components of capital (equipment, structures, and so on). His work on index number theory allowed one to reinterpret the Solow (1957) approach as an application of modern (Tornqvist-Divisia) index formulas and to extend their use to the empirically relevant, multiple output–multiple input case.[6] My earlier econometric work showed how to adjust for quality change, that failure to do so resulted in potentially large upward biases in the "official" investment goods deflators (causing economists to "overdeflate" capital growth and thus to overstate true productivity growth), and that education (and more generally labor quality) contributed to productivity growth and thus needed to be taken into account when computing the "residual."

There was a certain youthful recklessness in the Jorgenson-Griliches paper that announced, with a "Look Ma! No hands!" attitude, an almost complete "explanation" of the residual based on correcting various measurement errors in the standard ways of doing things. The people who had worked hard and gotten the field to where it was then were not amused.[7] In particular, Denison (1969) took the paper apart, brick by brick, and found a number of inconsistencies and some downright errors. He was especially critical of our procedures to adjust the measured growth in capital for changes in the rate of capital utilization (since it is "utilized capital" that contributes to output), arguing that we applied it too widely across the whole economy, including even residential housing! By the time we corrected our work and replied (Jorgenson and Griliches 1972), the explained portion of the conventional residual had shrunk from 94 percent to 46 percent, and our claim that we could do it all, without mirrors, had gone with it.

I still believe that we were right in our basic idea that productivity growth should be "explained" rather than just measured, and that errors of measurement and concept have a major role in this. But we did not go far enough in that direction. We tried to stick with the conventional framework of constant returns, competitive output and factor markets, and no externalities, offering improvements in index number formulas, a reweighting of capital input components, a measure of labor quality change, and improvements in the measurement of capital prices and utilization. It became clear, however, that a "full explanation" could not be achieved within the conventional framework without invoking increasing returns to scale, R&D spillovers, and other externalities and disequilibria. Whether such an extension is quantitatively feasible and whether it would do "enough" to explain the more recent slowdowns in productivity growth in the 1970s and 1980s remains to be seen.

The necessity of expanding the framework is perhaps seen easiest in the case of the contribution of education (human capital) to economic growth. In the Griliches-Jorgenson (1966, 1967) framework, human capital was an outside force, a costless input being added to the private economy. But once one expands the national accounts to include an educational sector that uses real resources to produce this capital good, as in Jorgenson and Fraumeni (1992a,b), and adds it also to the output side, it becomes just another capital investment opportunity that can generate *long-term* growth only if there are externalities and no diminishing returns in its production (Lucas 1993). However, investments in education can generate significant intermediate-term growth (which may last a long time) by eliminating the constraints imposed on such investments by imperfect capital markets, including capital rationing and the inability to pledge one's future human capital as a security for the necessary loans to finance such investments.

MOVING OUTSIDE THE CONVENTIONAL FRAMEWORK

It was no surprise to me, given my earlier work on the diffusion of technology and agricultural productivity (e.g., Griliches 1957), that one needed to step outside the conventional framework, that productivity growth represents the reaping of returns generated by knowledge production and its diffusion within and outside firms and industries. Its essence is the exploitation of new investment opportunities, in the form of new techniques, new products and markets, and new methods of organization and communication, and the associated increasing returns opportunities that such developments, including the growth of the economy as a whole, open up. Most of such growth can be thought of as arising endogenously, from the investment of economic resources in the diffusion of new technologies, in their "embodiment" in physical and human capital, in migration processes, and in R&D investments. All these are economic processes subject to economic analysis, but they did not fit comfortably within the straitjacket of conventional theory. Somehow, my training as an agricultural economist made me value the importance of markets and economic incentives but also made me comfortable with the possibility that much of the world is not in continuous, perfectly anticipated equilibrium. So I went on to pursue more detailed studies of what I still think are the major sources of growth— education (see, e.g., Griliches 1970 and 1977), increasing returns to scale (Griliches and Ringstad 1971), and R&D (Griliches 1973, 1980a,b, and 1986b)—leaving the conventional framework behind and with it *any* attempt at one, overarching "explanation."

Even though we economists now have more data, more advanced econometric techniques, and better computer resources, the overall state of the field has not advanced all that much in the last twenty-five years or so. We have a better understanding of the role played by increasing returns and human capital and more extensive quality adjustments in price indexes required to measure capital. Yet we are not that much closer to an "explanation" of the observed changes in the various productivity indexes (see Table 2.2 for a selected listing of recent numbers). A tremendous effort was launched by Jorgenson and his co-workers—Christensen, Fraumeni, Gollop, Nishimizu, and others—to improve and systemize the relevant data sources, to produce a consistent set of industry-level total factor productivity accounts, to extend and generalize our original labor quality adjustments, and to extend it also to international comparisons of productivity (see, e.g., Jorgenson, Gollop, and Fraumeni 1987 and Jorgenson 1990). At the same time, Denison was also refining his approach (Denison 1974 and 1984), and the U.S. government's Bureau of Labor Statistics (BLS) began to compute and publish official multifactor productivity indexes of its own (BLS 1983). But the incompleteness of all these approaches and the unsatisfactory state of this field as a whole was revealed by the sharp and prolonged slowdown in the growth of measured productivity that began in the late 1960s or early 1970s. Despite the best effort of these and other researchers, it has not proven possible to account for this slowdown within the standard growth accounting framework without concluding that the residual had changed, that the underlying total factor productivity growth had fallen (see Denison 1984, Griliches 1988b, Kendrick 1983, and many others).

Before one accepts this possibility as a fact, one needs to take another, more careful look at the measurement issues. It is my hunch that at least part of what happened is that the economy and its various technological thrusts moved into sectors and areas in which our measure-

Table 2.2. Selected recent estimates of the residual.

| | | | GROWTH RATES | |
| | | OUTPUT/ | CONVENTIONAL | ADJUSTED |
SOURCE	PERIOD	LABOR	RESIDUAL	RESIDUAL
	Total Private Economy			
Denison (1985)	1929–82	2.1	1.9	.6
Jorgenson-Fraumeni (1992a)	1948–73	2.9	1.4	1.3
	1973–79	1.7	.4	.2
	1979–87	2.2	1.2	.7
Jorgenson-Yip (1999)	1960–73	3.4	2.1	1.4
	1973–79	2.2	.9	.2
	1979–95	1.8	.9	.5
BLS (1999)	1948–73	3.3	2.3	2.1
	1973–79	1.3	.5	.5
	1979–97	1.2	.6	.3
	Agriculture			
Jorgenson-Gollop (1992)	1947–85	2.7	2.1	1.6
	1979–85			3.6
BLS (1991)	1948–90	5.0	2.9	
	1979–90	6.3	4.2	
USDA (1991)	1947–79	5.9	2.0	
	1979–85	1.7	3.4	
	1985–89	4.3	2.0	
USDA (1991)	1948–85		1.5	
	1979–85		3.4	
	1985–90		1.3	
Huffman-Evenson (1993)	1950–82		2.0	1.0
crops, livestock	1950–82		1.6	.3

ments of output are especially poor: services, information activities, health, and also the underground economy.[8] If one looks inside the U.S. economy, almost all the persistent component of the productivity slow-down occurred outside of manufacturing and agriculture (I return to this subject later, in Chapters 4 and 5). Much of it happened in services, but not in transportation or communication, sectors where output is relatively well measured.[9] This shift of the economy into less well measured sectors frustrates also our ability to better understand and measure the contribution of R&D, since more than half of all U.S. R&D is devoted to the defense, health, and space sectors with almost no decent measures of productivity at all. If technical progress occurs in these sectors, and there is every reason to suppose it does, our inability to measure output properly will lead to a downward bias in our estimates of aggregate productivity growth. Moreover, shifts in economic activity toward such sectors will accentuate the bias.

CAPITAL EMBODIMENT AS AN EXPLANATION

One of the first attempts to "explain" the movements in the computed total factor productivity indexes came in the form of the "embodiment" model, in which all (or most of the interesting) technological change has to be embodied in the design of new machinery and hence cannot be implemented except through new investment (Solow 1960). Thus investment in new capital goods becomes also the carrier of technical progress, and there is no progress without it. From our perspective of trying to explain the residual, the embodiment model implied that the conventional measures of growth in capital input would understate the true growth and thus lead us to overestimate the residual. The reason is that the investment goods price indexes used to deflate capital were not quality adjusted, and thus overdeflated new investment.

There were several theoretical and empirical difficulties with this model, plausible though it may be. First, the original version of the model assumed an exogenous constant rate of improvement in the quality of new machines, where the average level of technology lagged behind the constantly improving "frontier" technology, the distance being a function of the rate of investment. While the rate of diffusion of the new technologies depended on the rate of replacement of old technologies, the ultimate rate of growth of the economy as a whole was still a function of the exogenous rate of technical improvements in machinery. What made the model "work" was this assumption of a constant rate of such improvements. Jorgenson (1966) showed that without such an assumption the model was not distinguishable from one with disembodied technical change. Second, embodied technical change could only provide an explanation, in principle, if the age distribution of the capital stock was changing over time so as to give more weight to newer vintages. Denison (1964b) and Nelson (1964) questioned the empirical relevance of the model by showing that the size of the effects due to embodied technical change depended on changes in the average age of the capital equipment, which were, by and large, of a second order of magnitude. A number of different attempts to test the model at the macro level produced little evidence for it (one of the first was Berglas 1965). Capital was not a very strong variable in the aggregate production function to start out with, especially in the presence of a "null hypothesis" trend variable, and substituting slightly different moving averages of it did little to improve its performance.

The problem, of course, is not with the idea, which is clearly important and keeps recurring in different guises, but with the assumption of a constant, exogenously given rate of embodied technical change. One has to put something more into this model to get empirically useful results. There are basically two approaches to relaxing the assumption that quality improvements in capital occur at a constant rate. The first is to use hedonic regression methods to extend and reinterpret the idea of embodiment, letting the rate of capital improvement be estimated from data on prices and characteristics of new and used machines (Griliches 1961). A similar interpretation can also be given to the diffusion literature (Griliches 1957, Mansfield 1961, and David 1966) and to the more recent attempts to endogenize changes in aggregate production functions (Mundlak 1993). This approach is equivalent to using appropriate, quality-adjusted prices to deflate capital input for productivity measurement. Recent work along these lines has revived interest in the embodiment hypothesis, and indicates that embodied technical change may significantly increase the role of capital in accounting for output growth.[10] But the implied increased role for capital only deepens the productivity slowdown paradox. Moreover, this hedonic approach does not "explain" how capital improvements are generated, and so cannot tell us anything about the effectiveness of R&D and other inputs in producing embodied technical change. In this sense, the capital embodiment hypothesis remains an extension of growth accounting rather than an *explanation* of productivity growth.

The other approach taken to allow for capital embodiment at a nonconstant rate is to develop a model of how capital quality improvement is generated (e.g., by linking it to R&D) and to embed it in a conventional production function defined over quality-adjusted capital. Under suitable identification restrictions, we may be able to recover the "structural" parameters linking R&D to quality improvement and the conventional production function elasticities (see, e.g., Gordon, Schankerman, and Spady 1986).

A number of other attempts have been made to provide physical capital with a larger role. In Jorgenson and Griliches (1967) and in the subsequent work by Jorgenson and his associates, the role of capital is larger because the dependent variable is GNP (gross national product) rather than NNP (net national product), so the weight given to capital, which depends on the cost of capital, includes also depreciation and obsolescence (and also because consumer durables purchases are capitalized and their service flow added to both sides of the equation). This is more of a semantic rather than a real difference, however. The relative role of capital is larger and the relative role of the "residual" is smaller, but the actual unexplained amount of output growth is the same: it is only divided by a larger denominator. In the same vein, the recent larger estimates for the role of capital in output growth (e.g., by De Long and Summers 1991) are actually bad news in terms of explaining the residual. The larger role for capital does not come from an increase in its absolute contribution, but from the decline in both the growth of output and the growth of the residual. While the relative amount of growth "explained" by capital rises, the mystery actually deepens.

Econometric efforts to provide some empirical underpinnings for a larger role for physical capital have not been particularly successful. In my own work (Griliches 1994) explaining total factor productivity growth for 143 manufacturing industries from 1958 to 1989, I tried allowing the output elasticity coefficient on capital to be different from its measured factor share, which is the restriction that the computation of the residual imposes. But when I allowed the data to identify the appropriate weight for capital in the regressions (e.g., by introducing growth in capital input as an independent variable to explain the measured residual), the data favored a smaller weight for it, on the order of one half of the original one, rather than a larger one. The same is also true of the data at the firm and industry level reported on below. This may be due, of course, to errors in the measurement of capital. The point, however, is that there is little empirical evidence that goes in the other direction, except possibly for the recent attempt to focus on equipment investment by De Long and Summers (1991). But their results do not appear to be particularly robust to alternative interpretations and recalculations (see Auerbach et al. 1993).

More recently, the "new" growth theories have revived the notion of "embodiment" in the form that has come to be known as the *AK* formulation. The "*A*" refers to the efficiency level in the production function (e.g., the scaling factor in the Cobb-Douglas form); the "*K*" here refers to the capital stock. The basic idea in these models is that capital investment itself can be used to improve the productivity or quality of new machines (and that diminishing returns to this process do not set in because of assumed spillovers across firms!). This setup generates, implicitly, a much larger coefficient for physical capital in the *reduced form* of the aggregate production function (Romer 1990, Barro and Sala-i-Martin 1995, chap. 4). Since the stock of capital is endogenous in such a formulation, one cannot test this model directly. When more careful attempts have been made to confront it with the data, it has been rejected decisively (see Benhabib and Jovanovic 1991; Mankiw et al. 1992). It has been largely abandoned by its originators, at least in the version in which physical capital investment plays the key role, but it is still alive and well (among some theorists) especially in formulations where human and knowledge capital take center stage (for a comprehensive review, see Aghion and Howitt, 1998).

If standard procedures underestimate the contribution of capital

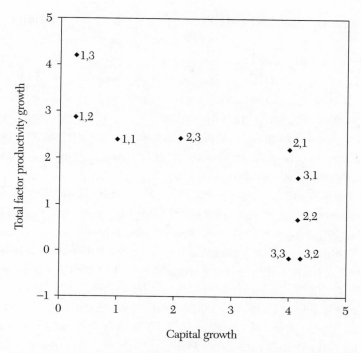

FIGURE 2.2 Total factor productivity growth (TFPG) versus capital growth, by major sector and period. The ordinary least squares regression on these data yields TFPG = 3.6 − .70 CG, (.17) $\bar{R}^2$ = .67. Explanation of data labels: Data points are labeled first by sector and second by period. Sectors: 1 = farming, 2 = manufacturing, 3 = nonfarm nonmanufacturing. Periods: 1 = 1948–1973, 2 = 1973–1979, 3 = 1979–1990. Point 1,1, for example, represents the farming sector from 1948 to 1973. (Source: Calculated by the author from unpublished BLS data.)

to productivity growth, then sectors or industries with a greater level of capital investment should also show higher measured productivity growth. However, this does not seem to be true. Figure 2.2 provides an illustrative diagram looking at three sectors in the U.S. over three time periods, based on BLS data. The evidence suggests a negative rather than positive relationship. Using Jorgenson's data at the 1-digit, ten-sector level for the two long periods 1948–1966 and 1966–1985, or at the more detailed thirty-five industry level for the whole 1948–1985 period, again yields no relationship across these industries between total factor productivity and capital growth or their deceleration. Similar results arise if one relates the more recent BLS estimates of total factor productivity (also referred to as multifactor productivity, or MFP) to the growth in capital services for nineteen manufacturing industries and three periods (taken from Gullickson 1995). The coefficient of the growth in capital input is not significant, either statistically or substantively. Either we need better measures of "true" capital change, or the story lies elsewhere, or both.

Recently some have suggested that the explanation is not that we understate the contribution of capital to productivity, but that the process of investment itself imposes short-term reductions in productivity. It has been alleged that, given the existence of substantial adjustment costs and the lag between investment and its contribution to output, large investments induced by major technical changes can have significant negative effects on *(concurrent)* productivity, thus explaining the large productivity decline around 1974 (see, e.g., Greenwood and Yorukoglu 1997 and Jovanovic 1997a). Even if adjustment costs are large, the explanation is not very plausible, since technologies diffuse very slowly and unevenly and are unlikely to produce such specific (high-frequency), visible effects. Moreover, capital investment did not accelerate much around that time, or later.

In short, attempts to explain the residual by adjusting the weight on capital have been widely tried, but without much success. I think that it is more fruitful to look elsewhere for the explanation, especially at investments in human capital and R&D, and the spillovers from these activities, which have been particularly emphasized in the "new" growth theories. These are the subjects of the next two chapters.

3

The Role of Education and Human Capital

When the early "growth accountants" such as Fabricant (1954), Abramovitz (1956), Kendrick (1956), and Solow (1957) found that most of the observed economic growth was not explained by conventional labor and capital measures, they pointed directly at the possibility that the changing quality of the labor force may be an important component of the explanation for the appearance of this "residual." The notion of investment in human capital as a major factor behind wage and income differences has a long history, going back to Adam Smith and before. The conceptual basis for much of the modern empirical work was laid down in the work by Friedman and Kuznets (1945) on measuring the returns to education for professional workers. The availability of detailed earnings-by-schooling data from the 1940 and 1950 Censuses made possible Mincer's (1958) pathbreaking contribution, which developed a framework for measuring the private returns to schooling (and related work by Houthakker 1959 and Miller 1960). The emphasis of most of this work, and the later but most influential work by Becker (1962), was primarily on the role of education in explaining aspects of the personal income distribution. It was Schultz (1960) who, I think, first connected this work with the puzzle of the "residual." He made an estimate of the growth in total human capital in the United States created by the educational system and estimated that it accounted for about one fifth of the growth in output.

A more direct way of adjusting the labor input for quality change due to the changing educational attainment of the labor force is to create a "weighted" measure of labor input, weighting different types (levels of schooling) of labor by their relative wages in the marketplace. This approach fits well with the overall national accounting scheme where different outputs and different investments are weighted in proportion to their prices. The idea is quite obvious. Its first implementation was actually in the context of industry wage differentials by Kendrick (1956), whose results implied a disequilibrium in the use of labor across industries and a gain in productivity from shifts in employment from low-wage to higher-wage industries. But this type of adjustment is more relevant for characteristics of individuals rather than the characteristics of their jobs. Working independently, both I (Griliches 1960a) and Denison (1962) produced estimates of quality change in labor input, using data on the changing distribution of the workforce by educational attainment and mean income by education as weights. My work on such labor quality indexes was extended to manufacturing in Griliches (1967) and to the economy as a whole in Jorgenson and Griliches (1967). It was continued subsequently by Jorgenson and his associates (see especially Chinloy 1980 and Jorgenson and Pachon 1983). More recent estimates can be found in BLS (1993) and Jorgenson, Ho, and Fraumeni (1994). The basic finding, both in Denison and Jorgenson-Griliches, was that such educational improvements in the U.S. labor force accounted at that time for about one third of the calculated *residual TFP,* or about a 0.5 percent per year contribution to the growth rate of aggregate output.[1] This contribution declined to about 0.2–0.3 percent per year in the more recent decades, but a similar decline occurred in measured TFP growth, leaving the fraction accounted for by educational improvements in the labor force at about the same level as before.

A most interesting recent development has been the series of new estimates of human capital produced by Jorgenson and Fraumeni

(1992a,b). As distinct from Schultz's original computations, their estimates are based on the present value of the increments in the future income flows produced by the educational system, rather than on its costs. This provides a relevant output measure for the educational sector and opens up the possibility of computing its changing productivity over time. But it also highlights the fact that, once incorporated into a wider definition of GDP, one which includes also the investment in human capital, "education" and the improvements in the quality of the labor force will become "inside," or produced, inputs. Then one will not be able to use them to account for the growth in overall factor productivity, since they are already netted out, except to the extent that the social returns to such investments may exceed the private ones, both because of the possibility of capital rationing constraints and because of the indirect externalities produced by education and the associated scientific enterprises.

This measure of educational output captures only the private returns to the educational investments and does not reflect any externalities created by it. Moreover, since directly computed private returns to education in the United States have not been very high and not been much above the discount rate used in such human capital constructions, a direct productivity calculation for the educational system as a whole that includes also the social cost of education (the publicly supported school and university expenditures) is likely to show declines in productivity and cannot be a "source of growth" on its own. Possible rehabilitations of "education" as a source of growth would include assigning large fractions of it to private consumption and to the maintenance and replacement of the stock of existing private and social human capital, only a smaller fraction of it being "net investment," though the whole activity may be a source of potential externalities.

Two major assumptions underlie such labor quality computations: (1) differences in earnings correspond to differences in contribution (marginal products) to national and sectoral outputs; and (2) these differences are in fact due to schooling and not to other factors such as native ability or family background that happen to be correlated with schooling. These assumptions are obviously controversial and were challenged from many directions. Feeling uneasy with "adjustments" for which there was no direct econometric evidence led me to pursue a number of studies whose main purpose was to investigate the validity of such labor quality adjustments. I will first discuss studies aimed at circumventing the assumption that differences in earnings reflect differences in marginal products, and then turn to the issue of "ability bias."

The main, and possibly only, approach to testing the productivity of schooling directly is to include it as a separate variable in an estimated production function. If one defines a weighted schooling-based labor quality index and includes it multiplicatively in a Cobb-Douglas production function framework, one has the additional implication that the coefficient of such an index should equal, approximately, the coefficient of labor quantity. This was the rationale behind a series of such studies that I pursued, both in agriculture and manufacturing. The results of these studies, summarized in Griliches (1970, table 4), supported the productivity interpretation: the schooling index coefficients were both statistically "significant" and of the right order of magnitude. Much of the subsequent work that was done along these lines was done on agricultural sector data from various developing countries with largely similar results (see Jamison and Lau 1982 for a survey). Table 3.1 summarizes the findings from a recent example of such work using data on Israeli manufacturing firms (Griliches and Regev 1995). The inclusion of a quality of labor index, based on the occupational distribution of a firm's labor force, contributes significantly to an explanation of inter-firm differences in productivity.[2] The production function approach provided *direct* and, to my mind, the best evidence on the productivity of education without using the a priori assertion that wage differences are proportional to marginal products.

SIGNALING, ABILITY BIAS, AND OTHER PROBLEMS

This work on the productivity of schooling actually anticipated and responded to a strand of criticism which was to arise later on under the la-

Table 3.1. Production function estimates for Israeli industrial firms, 1979, 1982, 1985, 1988 (dependent variable: production [gross] per person/year).

	LEVELS: POOLED, FULL SAMPLE (N = 7,742)			GROWTH RATES: POOLED (N = 5,018)	
	UNWEIGHTED	WEIGHTED		UNWEIGHTED	WEIGHTED
Intermediate inputs	.69	.68		.66	.74
	(157)	(148)		(83)	(95)
Capital services	.06	.06		.05	.02
	(11)	(12)		(4)	(1)
Labor quality	.41	.74		.14	.66
	(7)	(14)		(1)	(6)
R&D services	.03	.04		.04	.03
	(5)	(10)		(2)	(3)
Year 1982	−.02	.01	1979–82	.02	.03
	(−2)	(.1)		(2)	(6)
Year 1985	−.07	−.02	1982–85	.00	.01
	(−7)	(−2)			
Year 1988	−.05	.06	1985–88	.02	.05
	(−5)	(6)			

Source: Griliches (1997, table 1, p. S333, which was adapted from Griliches and Regev 1995, tables 5 and 7).

Note: Coefficients are given; *t*-ratios are in parentheses. The regressions contain also, in addition to the intercept, dummy variables for scale, sector, branch, life cycle status, mobility, and R&D status.

bel of "signaling" (Spence 1974), a theory which in its extreme form argued that the returns to schooling could be due to the informational content in the degree in sorting students, even if education had no real productivity effects. In effect, the theory claimed that there would be no returns to schooling per se, only returns to ability. In addition to the direct evidence from production functions, there is also quite a bit of *indirect* evidence against the empirical importance of "screening" or "signaling" as major determinants of the returns to schooling.[3] If the returns to schooling were largely due to the informational content of the certificate and not to the process of schooling itself, one would expect (1) that cheaper ways of testing would be developed by employers and employees; (2) that returns to schooling would be lower or nonexistent among farmers and other self-employed people, since they cannot collect on a false signal (Wolpin 1977); and (3) that the returns to schooling should decline with age as more experience is accumulated by employers about the true worth of their employees and the initial signal provided by schooling fades away into insignificance. But little of that is observed in the data.[4]

The most direct challenge to the original estimates of the contribution of schooling to economic growth was the issue of "ability bias." To what extent did observed income differentials exaggerate the contribution of schooling because of a positive correlation between native ability and the levels of schooling attained by different groups in the population? There were conflicting views on this in the early to mid-1960s, and it is still an issue that has not been fully settled. Denison (1964a) claimed, on the basis of very little data, that as much as 40 percent of the observed income differentials could be due to this "bias." This seemed rather high, and I embarked on a search for data that would throw some light on this topic. Starting with Griliches (1970) and Griliches and Mason (1972), a number of papers tried to estimate the magnitude of this bias using large data sets with army test scores (AFQT), IQ-type test scores collected from high schools, and data on siblings. The main results of this work are summarized in Griliches 1977 and 1979. They show that if "ability" is measured (albeit imperfectly) by test scores, the bias from this source is small, on the order of 0.01, as compared to point estimates of the schooling coefficient of about 0.06, and that it is possible that the bias actually goes in the opposite direction! If one treats ability as an unobservable which is related to such test scores and on which family members are positively correlated, then the unobservable that fits these requirements works primarily via schooling and has little or no direct effect on earnings, while the unobservable that is connected to the family component of earnings appears to have little to do with test scores.[5] In either case, the original estimates of the contribution of schooling were largely upheld. If anything, recent work has raised rather than lowered these estimates.[6]

One can think of "ability bias" as just another example of the "simultaneity problem" in economics: Schooling is not strictly exogenous. It may be related to the same unmeasured components of human capital that also enter into the disturbance in the individual's earnings equation, either because these components are rewarded in the market directly, above and beyond their effect on schooling attainment, or because they represent unmeasured variables in the future earnings equation forecasted by the individual but unobserved by the econometrician. To analyze this effectively one needs not only decent estimates of the earnings equation, but also a relevant model of the schooling decision itself that would provide the "other" equation for this system and indicate how other determinants of schooling might be used as instrumental variables to get a consistent estimate of its coefficient. Ben-Porath (1967) was the first one to set up the investment-in-schooling problem for the individual in a rigorous fashion. It did not, however, have a closed form solution. Using Sherwin Rosen's extension of the Ben-Porath model (Rosen 1973), I showed (Griliches 1977) that if one accepts the assumption of "neutrality"—that human capital is equally productive in learning and in the market—this implies that the ability bias is negative! Given that human capital accumulation is costly, those who start out with a larger initial preschool endowment of it, which is one simple definition of "ability," will actually invest less than those with a smaller initial endowment. To get a positive bias one has to abandon the neutrality assumption and allow for the possibility that this type of initial human capital is more productive if invested in learning than if it is taken directly to the market. That would produce a positive correlation between ability and schooling but leave little room for a bias in the earnings equation because of the low direct value of such capital in the market.

Recent work on this topic, using better twin samples (Ashenfelter and Krueger 1994) and better instrumental variables for schooling (Angrist and Krueger 1991, and Card 1995 and 1999), has reached similar conclusions. If anything, the schooling coefficient is underestimated within the standard ordinary least squares (OLS) earnings equation framework. The attempt by Herrnstein and Murray (1994) to resurrect the importance of "ability" (IQ) in *The Bell Curve* is largely beside the point, since it never considers the role of education explicitly, especially the component of education that is not correlated with the available test scores (see Goldberger and Manski 1995 for a review). There is some evidence that the role of measured IQ may have increased somewhat in recent samples (Altonji and Pierret 1996), but that may be largely a reflection of the same forces that have raised the returns to higher schooling in general.

THE CHANGING RETURNS TO SCHOOLING

The surprise of recent years has been the widening of educational wage differentials (see Murphy and Welch 1992 and many others). The increasing number of educated workers in the labor force should have driven down these differentials, as the earlier discussion of the "overeducated American" might have predicted (Freeman 1976). But it did not, despite continued worries about the declining quality of American labor, as reflected in SAT and other test scores. A number of only partially convincing explanations have been offered for this increase in the educational premium. The ones I want to mention are capital-skill complementarity (Griliches 1969 and 1970) and the technology-skill interaction (Nelson 1964; Nelson and Phelps 1966; and Welch 1970). The basic idea of the first was that, if physical capital and skilled labor are complementary, capital accumulation might explain the increase in the education premium, but the evidence for this hypothesis is rather weak (Berman, Bound, and Griliches 1994). The technology-skill hypothesis asserts that education becomes more valuable in periods of rapid technological change, and that it takes more education to cope with the ensuing upheavals and to figure out what is the right thing to do. The actual empirical work on this topic is not all that convincing, primarily because it is so difficult to get an independent and relevant measure of technological change.[7] Nevertheless, for lack of a more decisive explanation, the recent literature has attributed this phenomenon to the rising price of "skill" as the result of a technology-induced rising demand for it.[8]

The major facts are relatively clear, at least in the United States. The changing education of the labor force during the last fifty years has accounted for a significant proportion of overall productivity growth, perhaps as much as a third of it. But it has not accounted for most of it, nor can it explain why productivity growth declined in the last two decades. The rate of improvement in the average schooling of the labor force did not slow down significantly in the United States in recent decades, or in most other countries. Some have claimed that a decline in the quality of elementary and secondary schooling accounts for the productivity slowdown. One argument is that the quality of teachers has fallen, as measured by test scores, partly because of greater female labor force participation in traditionally male occupations and the expansion of the educational sector in the last two decades. Another line of argument is that the decline in two-parent families, the increasing prevalence of television, and other demographic factors contribute to a decline in the input by students into their schooling. There may be something to these concerns, but I do not think that these arguments can explain the rather sharp productivity declines that occurred in the 1970s and 1980s in the United States, Israel, and almost everywhere else. Moreover, as noted above, the private returns to schooling increased during this period! Whether the weights used in the construction of the labor quality index are just right or a little too high or a little too low does not make much difference, however, in assessing the direct contribution of schooling to growth. Changing the weight structure a little usually has only second-order effects in index number construction.

It is the case that, as conventionally measured, the growth in average education per worker is bounded, both mechanically, by the finiteness of our measures of schooling, and, more substantively, by the finiteness of human life. Even if one extends the concept of "education" to the more inclusive "human capital" and includes on-the-job training and learning by doing in it, still the rising opportunity cost of time and the fall in remaining time over which such investments have to be amortized would result in the cessation of investment at some point. That was one of Ben-Porath's original insights. Therefore, investment in education cannot be a source of indefinite growth in real income per capita unless one considers also the externalities produced by it in direct knowledge accumulation via investments in science and R&D and indirect effects via learning by doing and other knowledge spillovers. That is where the "new growth theories" come in, with their emphasis on how the externalities generated by R&D investments of firms and the human capital investment by individuals mitigate the diminishing returns that would otherwise limit the long-run growth rate.[9]

THE ROLE OF HUMAN CAPITAL
IN CROSS-COUNTRY GROWTH STUDIES

Recently a new style of econometric research has become popular with the public release of the Summers and Heston (1991) data on the growth experience of many countries. A robust finding of that literature is the positive contribution to growth of the initial average level of schooling, measured by literacy rates or primary and secondary school enrollment rates (Barro 1991, Barro and Lee 1994, and Mankiw, Romer, and Weil 1992). But what was rather jarring is the repeated finding, in these international data, that *changes* in the estimated levels of schooling or human capital do not contribute positively to growth, at least as measured over the 1965–1985 period (see Benhabib and Spiegel 1991, Jovanovic, Lach, and Lavy 1993, Kyriacou 1991, and Judson 1996). The explanations for this in the literature, besides pointing to the poor quality of the data, are not very convincing (e.g., see the survey by Jovanovic 1997a). They tend to focus on the embodiment of human capital externalities in new physical capital or in subsequent advances in knowledge and organization (Lucas 1993). But the estimated role of physical capital is not that large in these studies either.

I would like to suggest another possible answer to this puzzle, which is already implicit in some of the earlier work by Ben-Porath (1986) and Klinov (1986). Much, if not most, of the growth in human capital was absorbed in the public sectors of many of these economies. This is definitely true of Israel, where more than 80 percent of highly educated workers are employed in the public sector, in services, and in other "unmeasurable" (as far as output is concerned) sectors such as construction.

Approximately 60 percent of the total increase between 1970 and 1990 in the number of scientists, engineers, professionals, and technicians was absorbed into the public sector (see Table 3.2).[10] The story in the United States is similar, though the magnitudes are smaller (see Murphy and Welch 1993, table 3.5): 65 percent of the increase in the employment of workers with a college education was absorbed in such "unmeasurable" sectors. The role of the public sector was, however, much smaller in the United States; it took only 13 percent of this increase. But in many of the less developed countries, which make up the majority of the Summers and Heston data, the role of the public sector in absorbing highly educated workers is likely to be more, if not very, similar to what it was in Israel. This does not necessarily mean that such workers are unproductive in these sectors; they may indeed contribute a

Table 3.2. Employment by sector in Israel.

A. The employment of scientists, professionals, and technicians, 1970–1990

	IN THOUSANDS			AS PERCENT OF TOTAL GROWTH	
	1970	1980	1990	1970–80	1980–90
1. "Measurable" sectors	14.6	37.5	56.7	18	21
2. Public services	109.3	191.1	240.8	63	53
3. Other "unmeasurable" sectors	23.9	49.4	73.8	19	26

B. The employment of highly educated workers (with 16+ years of schooling), 1980–1990

	IN THOUSANDS		AS PERCENT OF TOTAL GROWTH
	1980	1990	1980–90
1. "Measurable" sectors	29.0	45.5	17
2. Public services	86.1	131.5	48
3. Other "unmeasurable" sectors	37.1	70.3	35

Source: Griliches (1997, p. S338); Israeli Central Statistical Bureau Labor Force Surveys (1970, 1980, and 1990), special series nos. 376, 690, and 912.

Note: Row 1: "Measurable": agriculture, industry, public utilities, transportation, and communications. Row 3: "Unmeasurable": construction, trade, financial, business, personal, and other services.

lot to the efficient functioning of the economy. But their contribution to productivity, and to growth in per capita real output, is not reflected in such data, because we have no good measures of real output for these sectors in the national income and product accounts of the various countries. At best, only their externalities could show up in the data, and that is unlikely, given that the estimated first-order effect of the size of the government sector on per capita income growth is negative! One does not have to be cynical to worry whether, in emphasizing the importance of education for economic growth, we may be somewhat self-serving, especially if we do not worry about the fact that much of the highly educated labor force winds up working for governments or various international agencies, and its subsequent contribution to economic growth may be problematic, at best. Thus it is not surprising that human capital change variables do not show up strongly in cross-country productivity growth regressions.

4

Estimating the Contribution of R&D

EARLY TECHNOLOGY STUDIES

The study of technology and technological change by economists and economic historians predates the appearance of the "residual" by many decades (see Singer 1954 and Usher 1954 for earlier examples and Mokyr 1990 for a survey). New technology in the form of railroads, cotton gins, electricity, the automobile, the telephone, radio, and much more was visibly changing the world. All of the major economists, from Smith and Ricardo to Marshall, Schumpeter, and Kuznets were well aware of it and discussed it as a source of both economic growth and tensions in the economy, well before there was an aggregate productivity index to connect it to. The students of this topic preferred working with "real" (tangible) measures of technical change, such as the diffusion of the tractor or combine, the spread of hybrid seed, or the invention of the transistor, and tended to look down on aggregate productivity calculations, when they appeared, as being too far removed from the subject at hand. The state of this branch of the field can be gauged by the 1960 Minneapolis conference "The Rate and Direction of Inventive Activity," organized by Simon Kuznets for the NBER and the Social Science Research Council (SSRC), and edited by Richard Nelson (1962a). Productivity measurement is barely mentioned in it.

But when the first "residual" computations were made and inter-

preted as a measure of technical change, it was reasonable to start looking at public and private efforts to produce such change for its sources
and explanations. Inventive activity and formal and informal R&D efforts thus became the obvious objects of attention. This was suggested
early on by Kendrick (1955) and Abramovitz (1956), while the first
"accounting" computations relating such indexes to patents and R&D
were made by Schmookler (1951), Schultz (1953), and Griliches (1958).
The first regression analyses with some measure of productivity being
related to R&D were done by Terleckyj (1958), Minasian (1962b),
Griliches (1964), and Mansfield (1965). Since then the subject has
grown enormously. I will not attempt to review all of this literature here,
having done it recently in Griliches (1992) and (1995). The size of this
literature can be gauged by the growing size of the bibliographies in
some of the better recent surveys. The Australian Industry Commission
(1995, vol. 3, app. QA), lists 27 studies estimating the returns to R&D at
the firm level, 28 at the industry level, 10 at the country level, and 20
studies for agriculture alone. Nadiri (1993) lists 50 studies. Mairesse
and Mohnen (1995) report 150+ studies relating R&D to productivity,
while Mohnen (1996) lists 59 studies focusing specifically on econometric estimates of R&D externalities. And more such surveys have appeared since.[1]

To the extent that the newly produced productivity growth numbers
required an explanation, the earlier studies of individual technologies
were not all that helpful. They taught one about the process of technological change and provided many insights but were difficult to connect
to any overall aggregate result, even in specific industries. Moreover,
they were very selective, sparse, and anecdotal, and often not in the
spirit of quantitative economics and econometrics as it was beginning to
develop then. It was relatively easy to think that the right thing to do
was to regress the computed productivity numbers on some measure of
R&D or inventive activity in the search for an "explanation" for it, treating R&D and scientific activity as another form of investment that cre-
ates a kind of long-lived "knowledge" capital. This was also consistent
with the notion that part or all of the measured residual is due to a

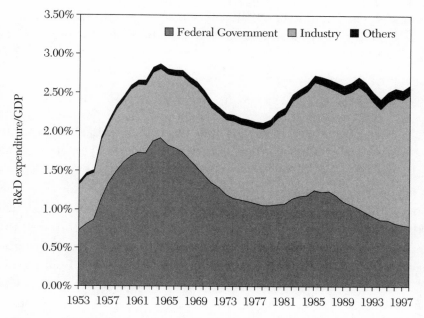

FIGURE 4.1   R&D expenditure as a percentage of GDP by funding source, 1953–1998. (Source: National Science Board 1998.)

misspecification of the relevant production function, due both to the mismeasurement of the included inputs and the noninclusion of additional types of capital, especially human capital (education embodied in workers) and knowledge capital, produced by public and private research activities (see Griliches 1960a and 1964 for early formulations of such an agenda).

Another problem in fitting the study of R&D capital into the macroeconomic framework of the early studies of the residual is the striking lack of time-series variation in R&D expenditures as a share of GDP (see Figure 4.1). This made it difficult to identify the contribution of R&D from aggregate data. As a result, attempts to estimate the rate of return to R&D, and its contribution to productivity, shifted to the microeconomic level.

This chapter discusses the analytical framework, econometric problems, and the main empirical findings from my attempts, and those of others, to use micro data to estimate the private and social returns to R&D and to specify the role of R&D in accounting for the productivity slowdown.

NONTECHNICAL OVERVIEW

Since this chapter is more technical than the others in the book, I begin by summarizing my main conclusions in less technical language. The basic model treats R&D as another "capital" stock in the production function, subject to an accumulation function that allows for "depreciation" in R&D capital. This approach has a number of serious conceptual difficulties (see the next section), especially its failure to incorporate the special features of knowledge capital such as the imperfect competition associated with its *production* and the increasing returns from its *use*. But the R&D capital model is a simple and tractable representation that enables us, at least in principle, to estimate the rate of return to R&D and thus to measure its contribution to productivity growth. In the section on econometric issues I discuss some of the problems that arise in such exercises, including simultaneity and measurement errors in R&D, and the techniques to deal with them. Despite the progress that has been made, I remain somewhat skeptical about our ability to find informative instrumental variables for R&D until we develop a better theory about the factors that determine the level of R&D investment.

The section on the R&D-productivity relationship reports on some attempts to measure the output elasticity and rate of return to R&D at the firm level. A considerable body of evidence points to a substantial private, and even larger social, rate of return to R&D. There is some indication that the private returns to R&D have declined (possibly because of increased obsolescence due to intensified competition), but no evidence that the social returns, or fecundity of R&D, has fallen.

One problem in interpreting estimates of the returns to R&D arises because R&D-performing firms typically have some degree of market power. Because output is measured at the firm level as revenues deflated by an industry (rather than the appropriate firm-specific) price index, we end up with an additional measurement error in the specification of the model. This misspecification leads us to understate the true R&D coefficient in the production function (see the section on identification). In effect, we end up measuring some combination of the underlying R&D coefficient and the degree of market power the firm exercises (as reflected in the price elasticity of demand). We need to bear this limitation in mind when interpreting our estimates of the contribution of R&D and how it changes over time.

Finally, I discuss attempts to document the presence of R&D spillovers. One approach is to infer spillovers from the divergence between the *private* rate of return estimated from firm-level data and the *social* rate of return estimated from sectoral or aggregate data. The other approach is to identify spillovers more directly by incorporating some measure of "borrowed R&D" into a production function model. There is considerable evidence of R&D spillovers across firms, industries, and countries. When we allow for these R&D spillovers, the decline in the growth of R&D capital can account for most of the productivity slowdown in U.S. manufacturing but only about half of the slowdown in the larger private economy, particularly in services where our measures of output are most problematic.

R&D "CAPITAL" MODEL

The R&D "capital" model (see Griliches 1973 and 1979 for early expositions) is still the ruling research paradigm today, in spite of its many weaknesses. Most of the applied work to be discussed here is based on it. It comes in several flavors, depending on how many such "capitals" are distinguished and whether the estimating equation uses stocks directly or is transformed into an "intensity" version (i.e., where the growth in productivity is related to the investment rate in this type of capital). Many different forms of R&D capital have been studied, including private, public, process as distinct from product-related, and

R&D done by "neighboring" firms or industries to reflect spillovers. The first, direct approach can be represented schematically by the following equation:

(4.1) $\quad \log Y = \alpha(t) + \beta \log X + \gamma \log K + u$

where Y is some measure of output at the firm, industry, or national level, X is a vector of standard economic inputs such as man-hours, structures and equipment, energy use, and so forth, K is one or more measures of cumulated research effort or "knowledge capital" by the unit and its "neighbors"; $\alpha(t)$ represents other forces that affect output and change systematically over time (I assume that $\alpha(t) = \exp(\alpha t)$ in the discussion below), while u reflects all other random fluctuations in output. The Cobb-Douglas functional form of this equation, linear in the logarithms of the variables, is to be taken as a first approximation to a potentially much more complex relationship. The focus is on the estimation of γ, the elasticity of output with respect to research capital. R&D capital is usually constructed as a weighted sum of past R&D expenditures with the weights reflecting both the potential delays in the impact of R&D on output and its possible eventual depreciation. (This construction is full of problems, some of which I will return to below.)

In the second formulation levels are replaced by growth rates and the above equation becomes

(4.2) $\quad \Delta \log Y = \alpha(t) + \beta \, \Delta \log X + \rho \, (R/Y) + \Delta u$

where Δ denotes a time difference, the term $\gamma \, \Delta \log K$ is "simplified" by using the definition $\rho = dY/dK = \gamma(Y/K)$ and approximating $\Delta \log K$ by R/K, where R is the *net* investment in K, net of the depreciation of the previously accumulated R&D capital. One can interpret ρ as the gross rate of return to investment in K, gross of depreciation and obsolescence.[2] In this form, the rate of growth of output or productivity is related to the intensity (R/Y) of the investment in R&D or some more general measure of investment in science and technology.

One can raise immediately a number of reservations about these skeletal "models." There are all of the difficulties of measuring output and output growth correctly in science and technology intensive sectors, there are issues of timing, depreciation, and coverage lurking in any construction of the R&D capital variable, and there are questions about which and whose R&D is relevant for productivity developments in a particular industry and whether all "R&Ds" should get the same weight in its construction. Some of these same difficulties reappear in trying to define an appropriate measure of *net* investment in R&D, net of the depreciation of the previously accumulated R&D capital. Probably the biggest problem with this "model" is its treatment of R&D and science as just another kind of investment, like buying a tractor or building a building. But investing in knowledge creation is not similar to installing air conditioning. It is rather difficult to measure the results of such activities and there may be aspects of increasing returns (nonrivalry) associated with the use of such "capital" that make it rather different from the other, more standard production function inputs. Nevertheless, this simple model is a convenient departure point for the discussion of some of the recent empirical work in this area and also for a consideration of several conceptual and data problems associated with its execution.

Early studies of this topic were happy to get the sign of the R&D variable "right" and to show that it matters, that it is a "significant" variable, contributing to productivity growth. Given the general scarcity of detailed data on R&D, this is still the main goal of many analyses, though occasionally the reach is more ambitious. Recent research has asked whether the fecundity of industrial R&D is affected by its source of financing (private versus governmental) or its type (basic versus applied); what is the role of R&D spillovers and how is one to measure them; how much of the growth in productivity can one ultimately attribute to R&D; and has this contribution declined over time? Recent research has also expanded into the international arena, looking for the direct and spillover effects of R&D on productivity across countries, time, and industries (see, for example, Coe and Helpman 1995, Eaton and Kortum 1997, and OECD 1996).

While the preponderance of the published studies shows significant contributions of R&D to productivity growth, both directly and via its spillovers, this evidence is more brittle than meets the eye. Like most empirical work these studies are subject to standard garden-variety data and econometric problems, many of which I have reviewed in the past (see, e.g., Griliches 1979 and 1995). In this discussion I will concentrate my remarks on only three topics: (1) the definition and construction of R&D capital variables; (2) the econometric problems caused by the endogeneity of such variables; and (3) the identification problem afflicting the construction of the various R&D spillover measures. The more substantive questions of the role of R&D in productivity growth and its slowdown and what the future may have in store for us will be taken up at the end of this book.

The standard approach to the construction of R&D "capital" is to aggregate (linearly) past R&D expenditures. There are several concerns with this assumption of linearity. It ignores the possibility that new knowledge production depends not only on current R&D efforts but also on previously accumulated results. Moreover, R&D flows as a source of additions to R&D capital may be subject to short-run decreasing returns to the intensity of search and to longer-run diminishing returns due to the fishing-out of technological opportunities, unless they are recharged by science or other sources of new discoveries. This is not a new concern. It is alluded to in Griliches (1979), it was raised in a number of papers by Evenson (e.g., 1984), and has been revived in a number of recent papers.

Formal properties of models where the change in the stock of R&D capital depends on the amount of R&D investment and the previous level of this stock have been considered by Bachrach (1990), Hall and Hayashi (1989), Lach (1994), Jones (1995), and Klette and Johansen (1996), among others. A reasonable version of such a model is:

$$\Delta K_i = R^{\gamma} K_i^{\phi} K_A^{h}$$

where ΔK_i denotes the absolute increment to the stock K, R is investment in R&D, the subscripts i and A stand for the firm's own and the aggregate stocks, respectively, the ϕ parameter associated with the own stock of knowledge reflects the within-firm spillovers and time interdependencies in the research process, and the h parameter, associated with the aggregate state of knowledge, reflects both positive external spillovers and negative crowding-out effects. Having started with such a model, one is left with no clear role for a separate depreciation effect, though some authors add a linear depreciation component to such models.

In estimation, such models lead to the "solving-out" of the unobservable K stock and the estimation of productivity growth as a function of R and lagged levels of output, TFP, or patent stocks. The current results along these lines are interesting but not fully convincing, both because of econometric problems associated with the use of lagged dependent variables, and because of the likely endogeneity of R, a topic to which I shall return below. The other major problem with the standard measures of R&D "capital" is that they are input rather than output measures. There have been a number of attempts to use possibly more relevant measures of R&D outcomes such as patents (see Cockburn and Griliches 1988 and Griliches 1990 for a survey) and other innovation "output" measures (see Crepon et al. 1997 for a recent example), but with only limited success.

Other conceptual problems are associated with the whole notion of "depreciation" of knowledge and with the question of how "knowledge" should be incorporated into the production function. Much of what we think of as depreciation is not "physical" forgetting, but rather the dissipation of rents as the result of obsolescence. It is a valid private cost component of innovation but not necessarily a social one. Its implications for measurement depend on the state of price index measurement technology and on the market structure of the relevant industries. In computers, where the incumbents have little market power, prices and revenues fall, but quantities need not. If correctly "deflated," there is little depreciation to knowledge capital in a "true" quality constant production function.

In pharmaceuticals, with incumbents choosing to depreciate their patent monopolies optimally and the appearance of new substitutes not causing incumbent prices to decline, "deflated revenues" will fall, and we would interpret that fall as the depreciation of private R&D capital (correctly) and a decline in productivity (incorrectly, since the same set of resources are still used in the industry, producing essentially the same quantities as before). All that has happened is that the previously accumulated R&D "capital" is now available to all in the industry and hence cannot collect much rent. But it is still contributing to the productivity (technology) of the industry. From a social perspective the loss of patent protection results not in a decline in such a capital, but potentially in even a rise in its utilization!

The fact that in most cases our micro production functions are closer to revenue functions than to true quantities makes the second case more prevalent than the first. But often our data are a mixture of the two, leading to great difficulties in the interpretation of the empirical results.

It is obvious that such capital does not depreciate just because of the efflux of time or mechanical wear and tear. The obsolescence of private R&D results is clearly a function of the activity of others and is unlikely to occur at a constant rate. A major challenge before us is to model this process convincingly. A start has been made by Caballero and Jaffe (1993), but this is yet to be transferred to the work on micro production functions.[3] In the empirical work discussed below, I use the "conventional" 15 percent figure for the depreciation of R&D capital.

The above discussion does not imply that there is no obsolescence in social knowledge. There has surely been loss in the social value of the knowledge stocks associated with making carbon copies of documents and shipbuilding technology. This is true in two senses: first, existing stocks are applied to much smaller industries, and hence the implicit social returns, the consumer surpluses attributable to the original invention of these products, become smaller as demand falls; second, they become much harder to retrieve owing to the lack of use, the retirement and death of associated human capital, and just plain forgetting. But such depreciation also does not have the usual declining-balance form (i.e., constant rate of exponential decay), except possibly in the aggregate, where the renewal theorem comes into play (Jorgenson 1973).[4]

The final set of problems is associated with the nonrivalrous nature of knowledge (Arrow 1962, Romer 1990). If the change in the stock of R&D capital is measured by R&D *input* rather than output, the question is still, "Should the resulting production function be interpreted as having constant returns including the R&D input?" The usual solution to this internal versus external economies of scale question was to treat the own R&D effects as subject to decreasing returns and include them in the standard list of inputs, while treating the spillovers from the R&D of others as externalities (see Griliches 1979 and 1992a), assuring perfect competition within the relevant sectors. If the change in the stock of R&D capital is to be measured by the *outputs* of the knowledge-producing processes, it becomes an index of the level of productivity along the lines of the quality-ladder models of Grossman and Helpman (1991) (i.e., models of imperfect competition with vertical product differentiation), and not simply another "capital" input within the list of standard inputs. In any event, the nonrivalrous nature of R&D results makes perfect competition solutions unlikely, leading to the patent system and other appropriability mechanisms and a divergence between price and marginal costs of production. This is undoubtedly true, but the implied increasing returns to scale may be less pervasive and more "local" than has been claimed by their proponents. First, much of knowledge creation is specific and compartmentalized. New grape-growing techniques may be only marginally useful in apple growing and not at all useful in banking. Moreover, such knowledge does not necessarily travel far and requires additional investments for its adoption and absorption (Adams and Jaffe 1996 and Jovanovic 1997a).

The recent revival in monopolistic competition theory and its application in this context make it clear that knowledge-producing firms will have nonnegligible markups, whose magnitude will depend on the conditions of competition in their industries and the strengths of their appropriability positions. What we have then in our data are revenue functions for which downward sloping demand functions "solve" the increasing returns "problem" (it is only a problem for our models, not necessarily for the real world). This has serious implications for how we estimate and interpret the coefficients on R&D capital, which are my topics in the next two sections.

ECONOMETRIC ISSUES

If R&D is chosen on the basis of economic incentives, it is unlikely to be fully independent of the shocks and errors that affect the production relations we are trying to estimate. This is the simultaneity problem. If all firms face the same production function and the same factor prices, it is not clear why different firms would choose different R&D levels. If they all do the same thing, we may not be able to estimate anything. If they do not, then we need to understand why not. That is the "identification" problem (see Griliches and Mairesse 1998 for a more general discussion of this topic).

The simultaneity problem refers to the possible confusion in causality: future output and its profitability depend on past R&D, while R&D, in turn, depends on both past output and expectations about its future. With long time series and detailed lag assumptions one might be able to analyze a recursive equations system with current output depending on past R&D, and past R&D depending on past rather than current output. In cross-sectional data with only a few observations per firm, it is much harder to make such distinctions, particularly since current expectations about the future are based on current and past data.

There are several "solutions" to the simultaneity problem. First, if one has good data series on the real factor costs of the various inputs, one could use them as instrumental variables for the estimation of the production function. Unfortunately, in the R&D context one is unlikely to have good factor price series. First, there are no published R&D

deflators at the detailed industry level. Second, if they were available, they would still be very highly correlated with the cost of labor and the cost of capital indexes, which are likely to be major ingredients of such indexes. What we will not have are changes in "real" R&D costs that we want to measure, in the productivity of such expenditures in a field or industry that are caused by various technological and scientific break-throughs. Even if one had the prices, they are likely to be highly collin-ear over time. There is one possible exception to this pessimistic view. With good data one could construct different "tax prices" of R&D fac-ing different firms, which could provide some relevant cross-sectional variation arising from differences in effective tax rates.

A second approach to the simultaneity problem is possible when both time series and cross-sectional data are available. If one is willing to assume a simple permanent-transitory model in which $u = \alpha + e$, where α is the permanent component that affects input demand choice, while e, the transitory component, does not, then consistent parameter estimates can be obtained by using the *within-firm* covariances. This is equivalent to allowing a separate constant term (dummy variable) for each firm, which would absorb the offending term, the permanent firm effect. But this covariance approach may exacerbate other problems, such as errors in the variables, which also afflict these kinds of data (for discussion, see Griliches 1986a).

Third, one may be able to find other instrumental variables of inter-est that may help to solve the identification problem in such models. Olley and Pakes (1996) present an interesting implementation of this approach. In the framework I am using, both labor and current R&D are endogenous, being affected by technological and other shocks. In a related model with only labor, Olley and Pakes use capital investment (actually, the part of capital investment that is not related to the capital stock and its higher-order terms) as a proxy for the technological shock. By including this (estimated) proxy variable for the technological shock directly in the labor equation, they "solve" the endogeneity problem. Of course, with two or more endogenous variables, as in the permanent-transitory model described above, more structure is needed in the system for identification.

The question whether the R&D stock measure is "contaminated" by simultaneity depends upon what is contained in the production function disturbance and to what extent it is *anticipated* by the decision makers (and thereby "transmitted" to the firm's choice of R&D). In studies of panel data of firms over time, the usual construction is to make R&D capital stock depend on past values of R&D subject to a constant rate of depreciation over time, that is, $K_t = \Sigma(1 - \delta)^j R_{t-1-j}$, where the summation over j goes from zero to infinity and thus puts *only* lagged (not contemporaneous) values of R&D into the equation. But to the extent that there are more or less permanent firm effects, reflecting market positions, differences in quality of the labor force, and other misspecifications, they all would also be correlated with past R&D decisions. Using only the within-firm variation, or taking first differences to analyze the growth rates rather than the levels of variables, eliminates such fixed effects but may still leave other specification errors, such as changing utilization rates and deflator errors. Also, current R&D decisions may anticipate some of the future shocks to the production function.

To do something about such current simultaneity and not just the simultaneity coming from the permanent differences among firms, and in the absence of substantive "external" causal variables that can serve as suitable instrumental variables, one has to lean more heavily on assumptions about lags in the transmission of the disturbances to the other decision variables and to use those lags as instruments in estimating such models (e.g., see Arellano and Bover 1995, Blundell and Bond 1996, and Mairesse and Hall 1996). For example, suppose the production function disturbance (which is serially uncorrelated) in period t affects R&D immediately but affects some other decision variable, say capital investment, only with a lag of one period. There is a simultaneity problem in estimating the R&D coefficient in a production function because of the contemporaneous transmission of the production function disturbance. But we can use capital investment lagged one period as a valid instrument for R&D, because it has not yet been "contaminated."

Consider a slightly more general model of the production function:

(4.3) $y_{it} = \beta x_{it} + \gamma k_{it} + \alpha_i + u_{it}$

(4.4) $u_{it} = \rho u_{it-1} + e_{it}$

where lower-case letters represent the logarithms of the variables, x is a composite of "conventional" inputs including capital, k is a measure of the R&D "stock," α_i is an unobserved permanent firm effect, while u_{it} is a randomly changing "technical" disturbance. Only the e_{it}, the "innovation" in u_{it}, is unpredictable and hence independent of current decisions affecting x and k. (Of course, u_{it} could be modeled as a higher-order auto-regression). In such a world, we can solve out u_{it} and rewrite the equation as:[5]

(4.5) $y_{it} = \beta(x_{it} - \rho x_{it-1}) + \gamma(k_{it} - \rho k_{it-1}) + \rho y_{it-1} + (1 - \rho)\alpha_i + e_{it}$

Therefore, we can use past *differences* in x, k, and y (e.g., $x_{it}-x_{it-1}$), which should be independent of the α_i's, as instruments.[6]

THE R&D-PRODUCTIVITY RELATIONSHIP

Tables 4.1 and 4.2 illustrate some of these econometric concerns in the context of my continued attempts to see if the contribution of R&D to firm productivity in the United States has declined over time (see Griliches 1986b, 1994, and 1998, chap. 12, for earlier efforts in the same vein). Table 4.1 looks at a select sample of long-term R&D performing firms and asks whether the estimated R&D coefficients changed significantly between 1979 and 1988 when we allow for there to be individual firm effects.[7] The answer is no. In the table I present estimates for regressions that allow the individual firm effects to be either correlated with the labor and physical capital variables ("correlated effects") or not correlated with them ("uncorrelated random effects").[8] The coefficients represent output elasticities with respect to labor, phys-

Table 4.1. Alternative estimates of production function parameters for U.S. R&D-performing firms, 1973, 1978, 1983, 1988 (standard errors in parentheses).

	UNCORRELATED RANDOM EFFECTS	CORRELATED EFFECTS	
	(1)	(2)	(3)
Labor	.686	.805	.818
	(.020)	(.029)	(.030)
Physical capital	.260	.062	.062
	(.014)	(.022)	(.022)
R&D Capital:	.065	.080	
Combined	(.015)	(.022)	
1973			.065
			(.024)
1978			.072
			(.023)
1983			.059
			(.024)
1988			.076
			(.023)
Chi-square (degrees	366	121	110
of freedom)	(45)	(33)	(30)

Note: Number of observations: 214 firms × 4 = 856. Minimum distance estimators based on Chamberlain (1984). Dependent variable: log deflated sales. Other variables in the equation: year dummy variables, computer (357) industry dummy variable, and computer-year interaction variables.

ical capital, and R&D capital. In the combined sample of years, the output elasticity of R&D is estimated at 0.08. When we allow the R&D coefficient to differ across years (the rows labeled 1973, 1978, 1983, and 1988), we find that the estimated output elasticities do not decline.

Table 4.2 expands and updates the sample significantly and looks at two subperiods, 1982–1987 and 1988–1995, estimating with the generalized method of moments (GMM), which allows both for potential simultaneity in all the inputs and serial correlation in the production function disturbances.[9] Because the instrumental variables that we (and others typically) use have little power, the results are less stable and somewhat dependent on the exact choice of time periods and rules for "cleaning" the data. The OLS estimates are provided for reference.

Table 4.2. Alternative estimates of production function parameters for U.S. R&D and non-R&D manufacturing firms, 1982–1987, levels (standard errors in parentheses).

VARIABLE	1982–1987, N = 676		1988–1995, N = 701	
	OLS (1)	GMM (2)	OLS (3)	GMM (4)
Labor	.616	.750	.623	.753
	(.013)	(.027)	(.013)	(.036)
Capital	.122	.289	.080	.114
	(.012)	(.027)	(.012)	(.027)
R&D stock	.041	.025	.053	.156
	(.012)	(.017)	(.029)	(.028)
Lagged output	.981	.573	.980	.816
	(.004)	(.023)	(.003)	(.013)

Note: The estimates are from the regression where I impose the same ρ coefficient in $(x - \rho x_{-1})$ and ρy_{-1}. Additional variables included in the equations: non-R&D dummy variable, year dummies, computer industry dummy, and interaction with year. Instrument sets: all differences as of $t-2$ and earlier, for l, c, k, and y_{-1}.

Again, we see that there is no evidence of any decline in the output elasticity of R&D. If anything, it rises in the more recent period, partly at the expense of falling physical capital coefficients.

The GMM approach uses the past values of the inputs and outputs in the regression as instruments. How much we need to lag these variables depends on our assumptions about how fast production function disturbances get "transmitted" to the decision variables and on the serial correlation structure of the disturbances. But what is the real identifying content of such instruments? The choice of inputs today depends on past demand and supply shocks, because, presumably, there are lags in adjustment and also erroneous decisions. But without specifying nontrivial real factor demand and supply equations with *measurable* exogenous shifters of such functions, we have no interesting variables that could be used to interpret (identify) their behavior. There are no measures of shifts in the potential demands for a firm's products, or of changes in technological opportunities and market structure, or of a firm's individual cost of capital. Without such shifters it is hard to tell whether the lagged values we typically use represent an interesting "experiment" that would allow us to identify something. Good instruments are hard to find without the supporting economic theory that gives them a formal role in the model, and fancy econometrics by itself cannot fix that problem. There is no substitute for a more complete model.

A slightly different approach, which also allows for individual firm fixed effects but ignores other sources of simultaneity, is presented in Table 4.3. It uses somewhat longer, four-year changes (for each firm in the data) to estimate the production function coefficients using the same framework as before. Taking these longer changes has the advantage of mitigating, by averaging out, the measurement error problem. The first part of the table is taken from an unpublished appendix to Hall (1993); the second represents my updating of this work. Looking at the estimated R&D coefficients we see that they fluctuate around 0.1, with the 1980s having a significant lower coefficient and a visible increase in the R&D coefficient in both data sets toward the end of the respective periods. What is more puzzling in such data is the relatively small and disappearing coefficient of physical capital. That may be the larger puzzle.

Table 4.3. Production function estimates for U.S. R&D firms, long differences.

| | | | COEFFICIENT (OUTPUT ELASTICITY) OF: | | |
	PERIOD	N	EMPLOYMENT	NET PLANT EQUIPMENT	R&D CAPITAL
Panel A	1964–70	112	.635	.153	.090
	1971–80	640	.805	.098	.069
	1981–85	960	.822	.150	.070
	1986–89	830	.739	.122	.152
	1964–89		.787	.124	.098
Panel B	1983–87	819	.704	.100	.027
	1987–91	712	.861	.007[a]	.020[a]
	1991–95	752	.833	.002[a]	.147
	1988–95	701	.809	.063	.088

Note: Panel A is from Hall (1993), unpublished appendix, table 2. Panel B is my updating of Hall's work using identical sources. Regressions include a computer industry dummy.

a. Not statistically significantly different from zero at conventional significance levels.

To summarize this evidence, when we try using various econometric approaches to address the simultaneity and measurement error problems encountered in estimating production functions (and other relationships too), we find no evidence that the output elasticity of R&D has declined since the 1960s. Thus the productivity slowdown cannot be explained by a declining weight on R&D over time.

IDENTIFICATION WHEN THERE IS MARKET POWER

Another major specification problem revolves around the implausible assumption that all firms within an industry charge the same prices. If product prices are both different and endogenous, then what is estimated is a *revenue* function, not a production function, with left-out product prices in the residual. This problem is considered by Klette and Griliches (1996), who build on an argument already made by Marschak and Andrews (1944). Suppose that demand facing the individual firm depends on aggregate demand and the firm's market share, which is determined by the substitution effects across products within the industry. In logarithms, we can express this in terms of symmetric demand (market share) functions:

$$(4.6) \quad y_i - y_I = \eta(p_i - p_I) + e$$

where y_i and y_I are respectively the real output of the firm and the industry, p_i is the firm's own price (or price index), $\eta < 0$ is demand elasticity with respect to the relative price of its own products, p_I is the aggregate industry price index (relative to the overall economy price level), and e is all other demand shifters for the products of this industry. Firm i's market share on the lefthand side depends on its price relative to its competitors. But suppose the variable we observe is not "real" output y, but revenue (sales) deflated by the available, *industry* price index. That is, in logs, $r_i = (y_i + p_i) - p_I$. Then, rather than estimating the true production function, $y = \beta x + \gamma k + u$, we are actually estimating the "revenue production" function:

(4.7) $r = \beta x + \gamma k + u + (p_i - p_I)$

There would be no problem here if the p_i's were random and exogenous. But if firms have a modicum of market power, at least in the short run, p_i will be set by them and will be correlated with u, x, and k (since technology shocks will affect the choice of inputs x and k, as well as the marginal cost and thus the price set by the firm). Klette and Griliches (1996, pp. 351–352) show that profit maximization, together with Equation (4.7), implies the following "pseudo production function":

(4.8) $r = (\beta x + \gamma k + u)/m - y_I/\eta - e/\eta$

where the "markup" coefficient $m = \eta / (1 + \eta)$ is likely to be larger than one (if $\eta > 1$ in absolute value). Note that the demand shock, e, has reappeared, because we have solved out for the (profit-maximizing) price. Since y_I and p_I are aggregate variables (common to all firms), we can "control" for them by introducing time dummy variables in the regression. Equation (4.8) shows that what we are actually estimating is not the true output elasticities of inputs but the elasticities divided by the markup coefficient. Therefore, our estimates of β and γ will be biased downward on the order of $1/m$. This means that we will underestimate both the true productivity effect of R&D and the degree of returns to scale, possibly implying decreasing returns to scale in contexts where there actually may be increasing returns. The intuition for why the price elasticity matters is that, when firms have market power, the way in which any increase in inputs will affect *revenues* depends on the price elasticity of demand, and thus on the equilibrium markup that the firm sets.

This identification problem also afflicts our estimates when we model the effects of R&D as shifting the demand function (product-related R&D) rather than reducing cost. Klette and Griliches (1996) show that if one assumes that R&D only shifts the firm's demand, then the R&D capital coefficient that we estimate, γ, is actually a measure of $-\phi/\eta$, where ϕ is the demand elasticity with respect to R&D and η is the price elasticity of demand.[10] Again, we do not identify the true impact of R&D on demand (in this example, ϕ). This result is exactly analogous to the case in Equation (4.8), where R&D lowers cost rather than shifts demand. If we generalize the model to allow R&D to affect both cost and demand, we end up identifying the R&D coefficient $(\gamma/m - \phi/\eta)$.[11] The estimated R&D capital coefficient is then a combination of its effects on both productivity and demand, attenuated by the price elasticity of demand. This coefficient can be rewritten as $\gamma + (\gamma - \phi)/\eta$, showing that the pure "productivity" effect of R&D, γ, will be underestimated as long as it is larger than its "demand" effect, ϕ (since $\eta < 0$). Klette and Griliches show that if one has a measure of the demand shifter (they use aggregate industry sales y_i for that) one can identify η, α, and β, but one cannot separate ϕ from γ, unless one assumes $\phi = 0$. Without actual individual firm prices, there may be little that we can do here except be more careful in our interpretation of such results. In particular, we may interpret changes in the R&D capital coefficient as reflecting changes in the fecundity of R&D when they might be due to changes in the average profit margin caused by changes in competitive pressures.

THE RATE OF RETURN TO R&D AND SPILLOVERS

Another way of looking at what has happened to private returns to R&D is to look at what has happened to the stock market valuation of a firm's R&D activity. In 1981 I found that the stock market had been valuing R&D investments at a premium relative to physical investments during the years 1968–1974 (Griliches 1981). Twelve years later, Hall (1993) showed that the market's valuation of R&D had declined sharply in the 1980s. Using the very simple assumption that the value of a firm V is equal to the sum of the valuations of its tangible assets A and its R&D "capital" K, we have $V = qA + bK$, where q and b represent the mar-

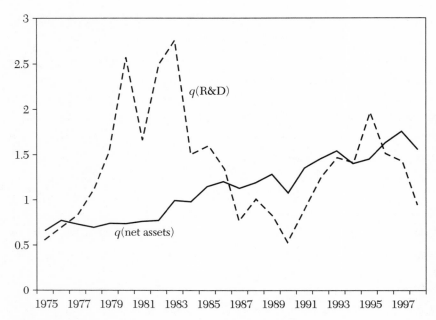

FIGURE 4.2 Implied valuations of physical capital and R&D capital in the stock market, 1975–1998. The underlying model is $V = q(a)A + q(r)K$. The plots present the estimated Q coefficients from the logarthmic form of the equation, $\log (V/A) = \log q(a) + \log (1 + q(r)K/q(a)A)$, using unbalanced annual cross-sections for the period 1975–1998. (Source: Hall and Kim 1999.)

ginal stock market valuation of physical and knowledge capital, respectively. Extending the earlier work into the 1990s, we get annual estimates of the q and b coefficients given in Figure 4.2.[12] They show a sharp drop, both in the relative and in the absolute valuation of R&D capital around 1985, with at best an erratic recovery since. This contrasts with the apparent recovery in the production function coefficients in the early 1990s, indicating possibly a sharp rise in the *private* rate of depreciation (obsolescence) of such capital, but not necessarily a drop in its *social* rate of return. This combination of high social rates of return to innovation, with high private depreciation, is consistent with a world of rapid technological change in an increasingly competitive environment.

All of this discussion has focused on estimating the effects of R&D, but what makes different firms choose to undertake different amounts of R&D? I have already noted the lack of good "external" causal variables. To the extent that differences in R&D reflect "technological opportunities," they could be modeled as differences in γ, firms facing (or possessing) different knowledge-producing technologies (though with the conventional input component kept the same within an industry). But unless one brings in some substantive variables that would explain this heterogeneity, such "generality" adds very little content. (See Mairesse and Griliches 1990 for a parallel discussion of heterogeneity in the physical capital elasticity.) The open modeling question is how to use the observed differences in R&D intensity to infer something interesting about the underlying sources of the heterogeneity in γ.[13]

The main thing that is missing from the estimates discussed above is an accounting for the left-out R&D spillover effects on both firm- and industry-wide growth in productivity. They are clearly very important but also extremely difficult to measure. The standard approach uses either an input-purchase (Terleckyj 1974) or a "technological distance" weighted measure of the research efforts of other firms within the same and/or neighboring industries or technological areas (see Griliches 1979 for an early suggestion of this approach; also Jaffe 1986 provides the first empirical implementation of the technological-distance approach). The input-purchase approach, which is the more common of the two, is based on the idea that technological change is transmitted to other industries in the form of quality improvements in the inputs they buy from other R&D-performing industries ("embodied spillovers"), if the prices of such inputs do not fully reflect the quality improvement. In effect, this approach "mis-attributes" the technical change to the buying rather than the supplying industry. The technological-distance approach is designed to capture the transmission of "pure knowledge spillovers" arising from the R&D activities of firms in similar technological areas (typically measured in terms of whether firms are patenting in the same technological fields or citing each other's patents). A significant amount of additional work has been done in this area since I reviewed it in 1992, much of it dealing with international spillovers. In Table 4.4 I list some of the more recent studies. They come in a great variety, but they all tend to find significant R&D externalities, with the median estimates clustering around social rates of return that are several times as large as the private or local ones (see Mohnen 1996, 1997 for reviews, and Jaffe and Trajtenberg 1999). But in a sense, this only deepens the mystery of the slowdown in productivity growth, since it is unlikely that the contribution of such spillovers would have declined in recent decades. The reduction in the cost of communication and the continued globalization of the U.S. economy should have increased the positive contributions of knowledge externalities, even though they may have also accelerated the obsolescence of the privately appropriated R&D capital.

While this work is pointing clearly in the right direction, it is subject to a serious identification problem: Do we get reasonable and "significant" results because a firm benefits from the efforts of the others or is that just a reflection of "spatially" correlated technological opportunities? It could be a response to common differences across fishing grounds, or in more technical terms, the individual firm effects α_i may not be independent of each other, but be subject to some "local" clustering, which will be picked up by the spillover measures. This issue is discussed in a more general context by Manski (1993), under the title of "the reflection problem." It would be nice if someone could come up with an approach that could distinguish between these two interpretations, but that is unlikely since the basic model is not identified without much more explicit restrictions and priors on the possible channels of communication.

Another way of looking for such spillovers is to shift one's attention to more aggregate (industry or economy-wide) levels, where some of the spillovers are internalized. In Table 4.5 I look at the recently constructed (by the BLS) multifactor productivity time series for nineteen 1-digit manufacturing industries (from Gullickson 1995) for four unequal subperiods: 1949–1973, 1973–1979, 1979–1990, and 1990–1996. I ask whether differences in the estimated rates of growth of multifactor

Table 4.4. Selected recent R&D spillovers studies.

SOURCE	COUNTRY OR OECD	WEIGHTING PATTERN TO CONSTRUCT "OUTSIDE" R&D	SPILLOVER RATIO (ESTIMATED COEFFICIENT OF SPILLOVERS) / (COEFFICIENT OF "OWN" R&D)
Plants and firms			
Adams and Jaffe (1996)	U.S.A.	Overlap in R&D patterns	5–6
Basant and Fikkert (1996)	India	Technology purchases	1.5
Harhoff (1995)	Germany (hi-tech firms median)	Overlap in R&D patterns	1
Klette (1996)	Norway	Other firms in same industry	2
Los and Verspagen (1996)	U.S.A.	Several alternative	14
Sectors and industries			
Evenson (1997)	OECD	Patents by industry of manufacture and use	n.s.
Hanel (1994)	Canada	Patent flows	Foreign: 1 Domestic: negative
van Pottelsberghe (1996)	Japan U.S.A. U.K.	Patent flows	0.7 4.1 5.0
Keller (1997)	OECD	Purchased inputs	Domestic: 8 Foreign, same sector: 3
Sakurai et al. (1995)	OECD	Purchased and imported inputs	n.s.
Sveikauskas (1995)	U.S.A.	Purchased inputs	1
Cost functions			
Bernstein (1997)	Canada	From electric products	4–10
Srinivasan (1996)	U.S.A.	Specific industries	1.4–5
Countries			
Coe and Helpman (1995)	OECD +	Bilateral import shares	0.5–1
Coe, Helpman and Hoffmeister (1997)	developing	Bilateral import shares	4
Frantzen (1997)	OECD	Import shares	2
Englander and Gurney (1994)	OECD	Purchased inputs	0.25
Park (1995)	OECD	R&D pattern	4

Note: n.s. signifies that coefficient is not significant.

Table 4.5. Multifactor productivity growth in U.S. manufacturing industries as a function of their R&D intensity (N = 19), 1949–1973, 1973–1979, 1979–1990, and 1990–1996 average rates of growth.

PERIOD	COEFFICIENT OF R&D INTENSITY (STANDARD ERROR)	PERIOD CONSTANTS	ADJUSTED R SQUARED
1949–73	.297	1.107	.150
	(.145)	(.153)	
1973–79	−.281	−.102	−.024
	(.369)	(.348)	
1979–90	.422	.778	.088
	(.255)	(.242)	
1990–96	1.187	.507	.158
	(.568)	(.527)	
Combined	.366	1.097	.269
	(.181)	−.232	
		.800	
		.834	

Source: MFP from BLS (1999); R&D intensity from National Science Foundation (1999a).
Note: This table reports five regressions, one for each period and a combined regression that uses data for all periods. The last four numbers in the third column are the estimated constants for each period in the combined regression.

productivity are related to differences in the R&D intensity. The answer is yes. In this R&D intensity form of the regression, the R&D coefficient represents the private rate of return at the *industry level* and thus contains the effect of spillovers across firms within a given industry. The rate of return should be interpreted as the "excess" return to R&D, above and beyond the return to other inputs, because the standard MFP computation already subtracts the "normal" contribution of R&D labor and capital included in the current inputs (see Schankerman 1981).[14] The estimated excess rate of return to R&D is about 25 percent on average, which is much higher than the rates of return estimated from firm-level production functions (around 10 percent), indicating the potential importance of R&D-related spillovers in the economy. There is some evidence in these data of a decline in this rate of return, but given the small size of this sample, it is not statistically significant.

Finally, I move to the more aggregate level and focus on whether

Table 4.6. U.S. aggregate multifactor productivity and cumulated R&D stock coefficients (standard errors in parentheses).

| VARIABLES | MANUFACTURING, 1956–1993 | | | PRIVATE BUSINESS, 1956–1994 | |
	TOTAL R&D	COMPANY-FINANCED		LEVELS	FIRST DIFFERENCES
LKRD(−1)	.124	.303	LKUSRD(−2)	.253	.182
	(.025)	(.059)		(.023)	(.065)
Trend	.008	−.003		−.003	−.001
	(.001)	(.003)		(.001)	(.004)
LCU	.308	.324		.161	.237
	(.047)	(.046)		(.079)	(.043)
AR(1)	.802	.767			
AR(2)	−.314	−.262			
$\bar{R}^2$	.994	.994		.956	.505
S.E.E.	.0107	.0106		.0245	.0133

Source: Multifactor productivity is from BLS, *Multifactor Productivity Trends* (issued periodically). LKRD and LKUSRD were computed by Griliches. Capacity utilization is from the Board of Governors of the Federal Reserve.

Note: The dependent variable is the log of the multifactor productivity of manufacturing and of private business. LKRD is the log of stock of industry R&D in 1992 dollars. LKUSRD is the stock of total US R&D. Trend equals year less 1955. LCU is the log of capacity utilization of manufacturing in July of each year, seasonally adjusted. (The capacity utilization of total industry was not available until 1966.)

The first two columns were estimated by maximum likelihood. The last two columns were estimated by ordinary least squares. All regressions included a constant term. For the first difference column, all variables were differenced and the trend variable becomes the constant term.

R&D can explain the productivity slowdown. In Table 4.6, I use the recent BLS time series on multifactor productivity for the U.S. manufacturing and the private business sector as a whole (including the services and farm sectors), and ask whether the rate of growth in multifactor productivity is related to the growth in the R&D capital stock. In this form of the model, the R&D coefficient represents the output elasticity of R&D. In order not to confound the effects of R&D growth with other time-related movements, I allow for an exogenous time trend, fluctuations in capacity utilization, and serial correlation in the disturbance. The estimated output elasticities of R&D are much larger at this aggregate level, on the order of 0.2–0.3, as compared to 0.1 or less at the firm level (see, e.g., Tables 4.1–4.3), indicating the potential importance

Table 4.7. Productivity and R&D stock average growth rates (in percent per year).

| PERIOD | MANUFACTURING | | | PRIVATE DOMESTIC ECONOMY | |
	MFP	COMPANY-FINANCED R&D STOCK	CAPACITY UTILIZATION	MFP	TOTAL R&D STOCK
1. 1954–1973	1.66	6.63	−.07	1.77	7.42
2. 1973–1979	0.33	3.50	0.29	0.67	1.40
3. 1979–1993	1.09	5.07	−0.36	−0.06	3.44
4. Deceleration (3 − 1)	−0.57	−1.56	−0.29	−1.83	−3.98
5. "Explained" by R&D	−0.47[a]			−0.72[b]	
6. Fraction "explained"[c]	0.83			0.40	

Source: MFP from BLS (1999); R&D intensity from National Science Foundation (1999a).
a. −0.303 (from Table 4.6) × 1.56.
b. −0.182 (from Table 4.6) × 3.98.
c. Equal to row (5) / row (4).

of R&D-related spillovers to the economy. The lag of productivity behind R&D implied by these estimates is about seven years.

My assessment of the contribution of R&D to productivity growth is summarized in Table 4.7, which presents the productivity growth rates for various subperiods and the parallel numbers on the growth of R&D stock and level of capacity utilization. I use the estimated R&D coefficients from Table 4.6 to evaluate the contribution of R&D to productivity change ($\gamma\Delta\log K$). Comparing the part "explained" by R&D with the overall deceleration in the table, I find that declines in the growth in the stock of R&D (not in its output elasticity) explain about 80 percent of the slowdown in manufacturing, but only about half of the larger slowdown in the private economy as a whole.[15] This leaves a major part of the productivity slowdown unexplained, particularly in the services sector, where output is most difficult to measure.

5

R&D and the Productivity Slowdown

In 1967 Jorgenson and I published "The Explanation of Productivity" paper. It did at least one thing right: it emphasized that productivity growth, as measured, is not a measure of technological change, pointing out many slips between the cup and the lip. It focused, in particular, on measurement errors in capital and labor inputs and on the wrong aggregation of their components, reducing thereby the relative role of the "residual," the unaccounted for growth in output. It came close to driving it down to zero before Denison (1969) found some errors and some overreaching in our work and drove the residual back to a respectable size again (see Table 2.1). Earlier, I had done even better for agriculture by "overexplaining" the residual there (Griliches 1963a, 1964). But even if we had been as successful ultimately as I was earlier in reducing the "residual," we were wrong in claiming that we had "explained" it.

Accounting is not explanation. It helps, and it tells you where to look further, but it was misleading to claim then that by decomposing the measured residual into its various components we were eliminating a major role for technical change in growth. (We were not claiming that explicitly, but we were not doing anything to dispel that impression either.) Implicitly, we were endogenizing parts of the residual, but we were not clear where they were coming from and whether technological change was involved in producing the various adjustments that "reduced" the measured residual. What we were pointing to was that much of the apparent productivity growth was not manna from heaven, but the result of economic activity involving investment: the improved education of the labor force and the improved quality of capital equipment. But the latter was clearly a form of "technical change," produced by informal learning, by design and formal R&D, and implemented by investment. In the end, an "explanation" must come from a description of such activities, their productivity, and the incentives they create for change in the rest of the economy. Our attempt at "explaining" it all away implied that there was no free lunch, that all growth required inputs, but it neglected to consider the possibility that some of the components may have higher rates of return than others or that some of the gains may not be privately appropriated. Nor did it describe how and why these improvements were in fact produced.

After the skirmish with Denison, the field settled down to an uneasy coexistence with the "residual." It was clear that some of it was being produced by the accumulation of human capital and improvements in physical capital but that a more complete accounting which also incorporated their contributions to the aggregate output measure would still leave us with a significant residual. The remaining residual is the result of various externalities: R&D and science spillovers, continued diffusion of technical and organizational innovations, and the elimination of various other disequilibria. All of these can be viewed as the product of private and social investments with above average rates of returns. It is the search for and the finding of such above-average-return investment opportunities that feed the growth in productivity.[1] And it was this realization that we would not be able to "explain" the residual without a better understanding of its sources which drove me back to the study of R&D and its effects on productivity, both at the firm level and the industry level.[2]

After the outcome of the debate with Denison, a broad consensus emerged on the magnitude of the residual in an overall accounting of output growth, along with a general expectation that the historical mix of input growth and the residual would continue, even if we could not "explain" the residual itself adequately. This temporary consensus was

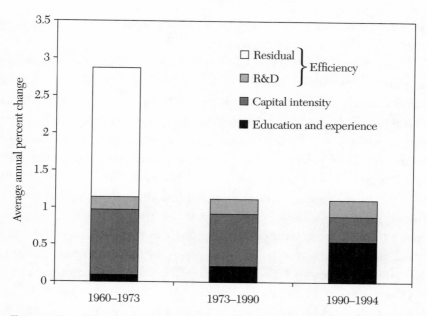

FIGURE 5.1 Growth of output per hour, 1960–1994.)Source: Calculated by the Council of Economic Advisers from data furnished by the BLS; reprinted from Baily 1996.)

shattered by the sharp and persistent slowdown in the growth of total factor productivity that started around 1974. As Figure 5.1 shows, the productivity slowdown was almost entirely due to the disappearance of the residual, which had still not returned as of the mid-1990s, whereas the combined contribution of capital intensity, labor quality (education and experience), and R&D was essentially the same in the pre- and post-slowdown periods.[3] There have been many reasonable attempts to explain the productivity slowdown (e.g., Denison 1979, Griliches 1980a and 1988b, Baily and Gordon 1988, and Diewert and Fox 1999, among many others), but no smoking gun has been found, and no single explanation appears to be able to account for all the facts, leaving the field in an unsettled state until this day. What I would like to do in this chapter is to review a number of the more interesting arguments about the possible sources of this slowdown and indicate what I think about them, and perhaps offer some tentative conclusions about whether the residual might come back. (First we wanted to get rid of the residual, now we want it back!)

The observed facts about the residual also influenced developments in theory. In particular, modern growth theory was built on the observation of significant productivity growth in the past and the expectation that it would continue into the future. The "new" growth theories "endogenized" this productivity growth by making it a product of the spillovers associated with the increasing returns aspects of knowledge production and the devotion of a fraction of the labor force to such activity. In these models future growth in per capita income depended on continued improvements in productivity. When the growth in productivity slowed down, future prospects for growth in per capita income worsened, and perhaps too the scientific value of these theories insofar as they did not seem to have any explanation for such fluctuations.[4] But productivity growth has always fluctuated, as Figure 2.1 showed for the longer term, and Figure 5.2 shows for a more magnified view of recent history. These fluctuations raise the question of whether such productivity indexes should be interpreted as measuring "technical change," something that presumably changes only very slowly and gradually at the macro level and does not experience many reverses. I will return to this point, that productivity change is not the same as technical change and vice versa, in the concluding chapter. But we should be aware of it as we interpret the data put before us.

A number of overlapping explanations has been offered for the facts depicted in Figures 5.1 and 5.2. The first is that the slowdown is mostly measurement error. This explanation takes two forms: first, that the correctly measured productivity may still be growing (Griliches 1994); and second, that productivity in the sense of efficiency may have declined in the 1970s in the United States and 1980s in Europe owing to oil shocks, inflation, and macro-induced declines in capacity utilization, but that efficiency decline need not imply any fall in the underlying rate of technical change (Diewert and Fox 1999). The second explanation is that the slowdown is real. The pessimistic version is that we are at the end of a particular technological boom cycle, facing the exhaustion of R&D op-

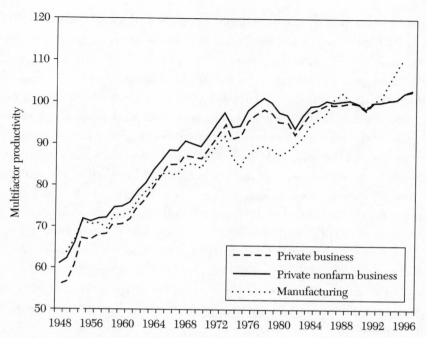

FIGURE 5.2   Multifactor productivity in the United States, 1948–1997 (1992 = 100). (Source: BLS 1999.)

portunities and a slowdown in human capital accumulation, and the future is bleak (Gordon 1999). The less pessimistic version is that there have been cycles before and there will be again and the future will be better (David 1991). The third explanation is that things are bad now *because* they are getting better. It is darkest just before the break of the dawn. Major technical changes are in progress, but this in itself *lowers* measured productivity because the costs of investment, adjustment, and adoption are very high (Hornstein and Krussel 1996, Greenwood, Hercowitz, and Krussel 1997, Howitt 1998, Jovanovic 1997b). Finally, there is the explanation that productivity growth will get (is getting?) better, but we may not fully appreciate it, because we will still not know how to measure it very well.

Now let us look at the "facts" briefly again. On the basis of the official BLS figures, a "slowdown" in aggregate multifactor (and labor) productivity growth may have begun as early as the late 1960s (see Figure 5.2) and this has led to several examinations of the data (see, e.g., Nordhaus 1972). But then growth snapped back smartly in the early 1970s, more than making up for the ground lost, and the Cassandras fell silent. When the oil shock of 1973–74 hit, it was easy to interpret it as a temporary real business cycle shock and expect a relatively quick recovery. But when the apparent recovery faltered in 1978 and the aggregate measures did not rebound significantly (and have not rebounded to this day), the questions became more searching.[5] Much more was really at stake. Of course, one can look at the facts in Figure 5.1 as a vindication of the Jorgenson-Griliches 1967 paper. In that paper we announced the program of "explaining" all of "productivity change," and now it looks like a complete success! Unfortunately, this "success" comes from the decline in the growth of productivity, rather than an expansion or a rise in its explanatory components. But what there is left is now fully explained by growth in labor quality and a modest allowance for the contribution of R&D.[6]

I will not belabor the measurement error story (see Griliches 1994 for more detail), except to note that most of the persistent slowdown has been occurring in sectors of the economy where real output measurement is especially difficult. Figure 5.3 illustrates this by plotting *labor* productivity (taken from the BLS) separately for the two groupings of sectors that I label, approximately, as "measurable" and "unmeasurable." The latter category includes financial and insurance services, construction, wholesale and retail trade, and health and other personal services (government is excluded, even though its output is also largely unmeasurable). Table 5.1 provides the underlying sectoral detail in labor productivity growth.

The productivity slowdown in the "unmeasurable" sectors can be seen also in the behavior of *multifactor* productivity (Table 5.2). During the 1979–1996 period, while multifactor productivity was growing at the respectable clip of 1.28 percent per year in manufacturing, in the private nonfarm business economy as a whole its rate of growth was effectively *zero!* This is only slightly unfair, because the aggregate numbers

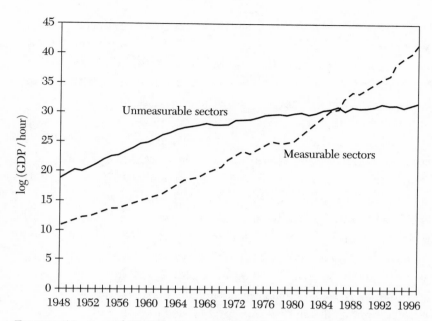

FIGURE 5.3   Log of GDP per hour, 1948–1996. (Source: Author's calculation based on data from the U.S. Department of Commerce, STAT USA website: <www.stat-usa.gov>.)

are adjusted for changes in the quality of the labor input, while the manufacturing numbers are not. If that adjustment is undone, the rate of growth of MFP in the nonfarm business sector during 1979–1996 rises from about zero to close to half a percent per year (0.47), only a third of the rate in manufacturing. But this comparison is actually even worse, since the published MFP numbers for manufacturing are on a "gross output" rather than a "value added" basis and are not really comparable to the national totals that are based on GDP. A comparable number for manufacturing would show MFP growing at about 2.2 percent during the same time period (Lysko 1995). Using this information on manufacturing and the total nonfarm business sector, I have computed the implied rate of growth in the nonfarm, nonmanufacturing sector to be about −0.1 percent per year during the last fourteen-year period.[7] The implied behavior of MFP in the purely unmeasurable sectors is probably even worse, since there has been significant productivity growth in air transport and communications, where our measurement is somewhat better. It could be the case that the productivity of three quarters of the U.S. economy has been declining for fourteen years in a row, but I doubt it. Surely there is a role for measurement error somewhere here.

Nevertheless, the decline in productivity in the "unmeasurable" sectors is probably not all measurement error. First, MFP declined also in manufacturing by about a third between the pre-1973 and post-1979 periods. Second, when MFP is computed separately for nineteen 2-digit level industries within manufacturing itself (see Gullickson 1995, BLS 1995, table 8), only two industries (machinery, including computers, and electronics) show significant increases in their growth rates between 1949–1973 and 1979–1993, seven are essentially unchanged, and the remaining ten have had significant declines. So the slowdown has been happening also in the "measurable" sectors!

However, these numbers bring up another puzzle. It is agreed that in many service industries we do not know how to measure output and that we expect zero productivity growth there "by construction," and that is what we get during the last twenty or so years. But why then was MFP growing in the nonfarm, nonmanufacturing sector at a rate of 1.8 percent per year between 1949 and 1973? And looking at Table 5.1, we see substantial growth in labor productivity from 1948 to 1973 in the financial sector (FIRE, which includes real estate) and in other services. What was happening then that is not happening now? Were we not improving our measurement methodology all along? Is it possible that we did a better measurement job then than now? What did we forget? Or are the earlier data, which may now be actually *the* puzzle, themselves wrong, and hence is the impression of the subsequent "slowdown" also wrong?

Having established that there may be something here to explain after all, let us now turn to some of the explanations that have been offered. The most interesting ones revolve around the notion that we have come to the end of a long cycle ("one big wave" in Gordon's 1999

Table 5.1. Labor productivity (GDP/hour) growth rates (in percent).

	1948–1973	1979–1997
0. Total: private domestic	2.4	1.2
1. Agriculture	3.2	4.1
2. Mining	4.0	4.4
3. Construction	0.3	−0.1
4. Manufacturing, durables	2.4	3.8
5. Manufacturing, nondurables	3.3	2.0
6. Transportation	2.2	0.7
7. Communication	5.0	3.4
8. Public utilities	5.7	1.9
9. Wholesale trade	2.9	3.4
10. Retail trade	1.6	1.6
11. FIRE	1.7	0.6
12. Other services	1.2	−0.8
13. "Measurable" sectors	3.1	2.8
14. "Unmeasurable" sectors	1.7	0.4

Source: 1948–1973: *Survey of Current Business* (January 1992 and May 1993); *National Income and Product Accounts,* 1982; 1979–1997: *Survey of Current Business* (November 1998); STAT-USA (U.S. Department of Commerce computer file at <www.stat-usa.gov>).

13 = 1 + 2 + 4 + 5 + 6 + 7 + 8.
14 = 3 + 9 + 10 + 11 + 12.

Note: Share of "measurable" sectors in total GDP (including government):

Year	Nominal GDP	Total man-hours
1948	.49	.47
1973	.38	.35
1979	.37	.33
1997	.28	.25

phrase), which was initiated by the pent-up demand during the Depression and the subsequent war and the accumulated technological breakthroughs and was sustained by the rapid diffusion of industrial R&D labs, fed by the vision of wartime successes of the Manhattan and other such projects and by a large infusion of government resources. The cycle came to an end because we eventually reduced the rate of growth of our investments in R&D and human capital formation (our fault!), or because the rate of return to such investments declined (the fault of the gods!), owing to the ultimate exhaustion of the opportunities that were opened up originally fifty to sixty years ago. These arguments are not new. Warnings about the coming exhaustion of future growth opportu-

Table 5.2. Multifactor productivity growth (percent per year)

	1949–1973	1979–1996
Nonfarm business excluding	1.87	0.13
labor quality adjustment	1.97	0.47
Manufacturing[a]	1.53	1.28
Implied nonfarm	1.79	−0.11
nonmanufacturing[b]		

Source: BLS 1999, p. 36.

a. Based on gross sectoral output measure rather than GDP.

b. The first number is computed as $(1.97 - .32 \times 1.53/.65) / (1 - .32)$, where .32 is the approximate share of manufacturing in total nonfarm business during the first period and .65 is the ratio of value added to sectoral output in manufacturing. These two numbers are approximately .23 and .53 respectively for the second period.

nities have appeared repeatedly. Particularly interesting and instructive is Jevons (1866) on "the coal question," predicting the decline of Great Britain as its coal seams ran out. Books have been written about "long cycles." Kuznets's first major book (1930) is devoted to documenting how the rate of growth of industries slows down as they grow older.[8] In 1960, Brozen was speculating that "there may still be room for sufficient additional improvements in research management to prevent diminishing returns . . . from slowing the rate of growth (in R&D) for a few more years" (p. 217). The question of whether invention opportunities are becoming "exhausted" has been widely debated, especially in the literature based on patent data (see, e.g., Evenson 1984 and Griliches 1990).

I look at the R&D story in somewhat more detail in the next two figures. As shown in Chapter 4 (Figure 4.1), at the national level R&D as a percentage of GDP peaked in 1966 and then declined throughout most of the 1970s. This looks as if it might help explain the productivity slowdown, except that most of the dip in the flow of R&D is coming from public defense and space R&D expenditures, which should not have had such a big effect on measured productivity. Nor is the timing really right. R&D does not have large immediate effects. It takes years for new products and processes to be developed and diffused before they are likely to affect aggregate productivity noticeably. Figure 5.4 plots a measure of industry-financed "R&D capital," lagged by two years, to-

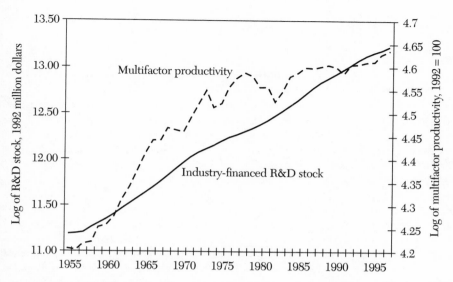

FIGURE 5.4 Multifactor productivity in the private business sector and industry-financed R&D stock (lagged two years). (Source: Author's calculation based on data from National Science Foundation 1999b and BLS 1999.)

gether with the index of multifactor productivity in the private business sector. The growth in R&D capital did not really slow down before the mid-1970s, while MFP was beginning to show signs of the slowdown already in the late 1960s.[9] Moreover, the growth in industrial R&D picked up significantly in the early 1980s and did not turn down again until the early 1990s, as did the growth in the quality of labor. Hence, if productivity is not growing fast enough, it is not because we have stopped investing in its improvements. Perhaps we are getting less for our investments, or perhaps we do not know how to measure the returns to such investments, especially since they are happening in new and uncharted fields.

I have discussed the question of the loss of "fecundity" of R&D in Chapter 4 and in a number of past papers (Griliches 1988b, 1990, and 1998b). The evidence is mixed (see also Hall 1996), but it points to declines in private returns to R&D in some of the older established research areas, but not necessarily in social returns. The active growth of

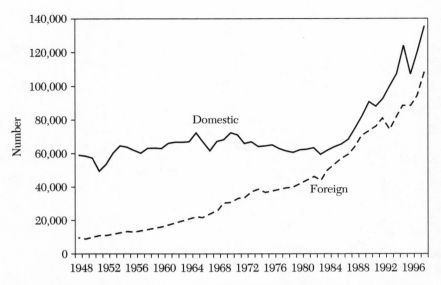

FIGURE 5.5   Patent applications in the United States, 1948–1998. (Source: U.S. Department of Commerce, U.S. Patent and Trademark Office, Technology Assessment and Forecast Program website: <www.uspto.gov>.)

new research-oriented companies in biotechnology and computer-related industries makes one doubt that we have exhausted our invention possibilities, and surely not the innovation possibilities looming in the future diffusion of already developing technologies. There are also more optimistic indications to be gleaned from Figure 5.5. After stagnating for almost forty years, patent applications in the United States (both those of domestic and those of foreign origin) have really taken off in the last decade. This "explosion" in patenting has been examined by Kortum and Lerner (1998), who conclude that it is not just a response to the better judicial climate but may actually reflect an overall expansion of technological opportunities or, at least, a decline in the real cost of inventing, possibly due to the breakthroughs in information flows and increases in computing power. So why are the effects of such an expansion of technological opportunities not visible in the productivity numbers?

There are several possible answers. First, "don't worry, it is coming, but it takes time for such big changes to work themselves through the system." Second, "it is already here but it has been very costly to pursue it and to adopt it, so the positive longer-run net product is still invisible." And third, "it is already here, and more is coming, but we do not know how to measure it (for example, gains from information and health technologies), nor are we likely to learn how to do so in the near future."

I am not convinced by the first two arguments. There is something to them, but they are unlikely to account for the big picture. It is true that most of the productivity gains from the breakthroughs in biotechnology are still ahead of us. But the computer and communications revolution has been going on for twenty–thirty years or more, and it is reasonably well diffused by now. Similarly, many of the adjustment and adoption costs should have been amortized by now. Moreover, measured productivity growth has also been slow in industries that are not in the information technology "mainstream" and have not been subject to the same intensive developments, such as the food, paper, lumber, furniture, and stone, clay, and glass industries. I am inclined to be optimistic about the underlying technological trends but pessimistic about our ability to measure them correctly. Knowledge, information, and health are all very slippery concepts, and our ability to measure the gains from such developments is still very limited.

The longer-run future of technology is more cloudy. We do not know what the next major areas of breakthrough will be or even if there will be any. It is reasonable to hope for the best, but we must also remember that invention is just that, something new that is not predictable on the basis of current information (or it would have been invented already). And economists are no better than meteorologists at predicting the future. Unfortunately, we still have problems explaining the past.

6

Reminders for Traveling the Research Road Ahead

A country which has been prosperous for a generation or two, acquires faith in the unlimited possibilities of economic development, in the inexhaustible opportunities provided by technical progress and the energy of its people.   KUZNETS 1930, P. 2

Our story started out with the discovery of the residual and the inability of our theories to explain it. We covered it up by relabeling it "technical change" and building growth theories around it. We also tried to "explain" it as the consequence of human capital accumulation, and of formal R&D efforts and their spillovers. But just as we built up the evidentiary case for our explanations, the growth of the residual declined significantly, requiring a new round of different explanations. The most reasonable explanation for the longer-run persistence of what started out as a short-run response to a real supply (oil price) shock is the character and location of the recovery and the technical changes that followed. The latter were based primarily on developments in information technology, a fact that makes them intrinsically difficult to measure, and were happening in sectors of the economy in which output and productivity are almost impossible to measure in the first place. This interpretation leads one to be a bit more optimistic about the future, as does also the more recent up-tick in manufacturing productivity and the evidence on R&D and patenting activity. But it is also true that these facts are shrouded in clouds of data uncertainty and that their extrapolation into the future is tenuous at best. While we may not know much about the future (did we actually promise that?), quite a bit has been learned in this quest for understanding. The process itself is valuable. Nevertheless, an unfriendly critic could look at the whole history of this line of research and be tempted to paraphrase Oscar Wilde's observation about foxhunting as "the overeducated in pursuit of the unknowable."[1]

It is reasonable to forecast continued growth in productivity in the intermediate run, as current innovations in biotechnology, computers, communications, and materials are perfected and diffuse further. But the longer-run future of invention is unforecastable. One can remain optimistic, but I do not believe that the gods of science and research either owe us or will necessarily deliver exponential growth. There is enough work left to do, however, for this and several more generations to come, to improve the world as it is, to move the "average productivity" toward its "possibilities frontier," and to realize the potential of the world economy as a whole more effectively.

I would like to end by emphasizing a few obvious statements that sometimes get lost in our rush toward modeling. *First,* productivity growth is not technical change, and vice versa. Productivity is also affected by the efficiency with which existing industrial enterprises and other social institutions are operating. It changes as the result of changes in capacity utilization, scale, organization, learning by doing, and more. Technical change is a change in how things are done, primarily as the result of changes in equipment, materials, and methods of operation. One can think of it as both the appearance of new blueprints and formulas (a shift in the production possibilities frontier) and the spread of the actual new products and processes that embody them. The latter, the diffusion of the best available techniques, has received too little attention in this book and in the literature overall. Also, technical change need not imply a growth in productivity per se. It could be the result of a movement along an existing "potential" isoquant requiring the use of a different piece of equipment. And the new equipment may not really be more productive, or at least not immediately.

Second, R&D is not the source of all productivity growth. Besides basic science, which does not fit the purposeful R&D mold, many productivity advances come from learning on the job and from informal attempts to improve production and distribution processes by the participants in them. Such "informal R&D" may be an important source of improvement, but we have relatively little systematic evidence about it or understanding of how best to promote it. It may be that informal R&D is correlated with private, formal R&D activity and thus captured by our focus on the latter, but we cannot be sure until we have useful measures of those informal activities. In any case, it would be unreasonable to expect our measures of formal R&D activity to account for all, or even most, of productivity growth.[2]

Third, knowledge is not a free good. It takes effort to develop it, to transfer it, and to absorb it. One of the major components of any research effort is *re-search,* trying to find out what is already known about some of the components of one's problem. Moreover, much of the available knowledge is highly technical and cannot be absorbed without specific and extensive training, and even more of it is tacit and not easily communicated even by the one who knows it. As Hayek (1945, p. 521) said, "there is . . . a body of very important but unorganized knowledge which cannot possibly be called scientific in the sense of knowledge of general rules: the knowledge of the particular circumstances of time and place." In this sense, models that treat all knowledge as both freely applicable and transferable everywhere are wildly optimistic.

Fourth, neither the world, nor the economy, nor the individuals in it are in continuous equilibrium. The opposite is the normal state. Individuals continually strive to change the situation around them, either because they are dissatisfied with it, because they think that they see opportunities for improving it, or out of boredom. But this unease, this human lack of *sitzfleisch* (Yiddish, which in this context means the lack of patience with the status quo) is a major source of the changes around us. Moreover, nobody knows everything, and therein lies the source of both inefficiencies and opportunities. "Any approach . . . which in effect starts from the assumption that people's *knowledge* corresponds with the objective *facts* of the situation, systematically leaves out what is our main task to explain" (Hayek, p. 530). The study of growth will require embracing more seriously a view of the economy where decentralized information and incentives in a constantly evolving world make all the difference. But progress will lie in merging those general insights with useful theory, careful measurement, and serious econometric work.

Fifth, accounting is not explanation. We can take a productivity growth calculation and allocate it in great detail to the various missed components, reducing thereby the role of the "unallocated" residual. But this, while very instructive and valuable, only shifts the problem to a new set of questions: Why was there all this investment in human capital? Will it continue? Where did the improvements in capital equipment come from? What affects the rate of capital utilization and the institutions within which both production and invention are pursued? It has been repeatedly noted that the aggregate production function is a structural relation, not a reduced form, and that one can solve out the endogenous reproducible inputs, such as capital, whose accumulation is itself a function of technical change, thereby giving the latter a much larger share of the ultimate story (Gordon 1968, Rymes 1971, Jefferson 1997, and Metcalfe 1997, among many others). But that is just another version of accounting and not a real explanation either. Real explanations will come from understanding the sources of scientific and technological advances and from identifying the incentives and circumstances that brought them about and that facilitated their implementation and diffusion. Explanation must come from comprehending the historical detail from finding ways of generalizing (modeling?) the patterns that may be discernible in the welter in it. This leads us back to the study of the history of science and technology and the diffusion of their products, a topic that we have left largely to others. But if we want to understand better what we are talking about, where technical change is actually coming from, we will need to study history. There is no free lunch in economic research either.

Sixth, increases in total factor productivity are not synonymous with increases in social welfare. Most reasonable measures of social welfare pay some attention to the distribution of income or wealth. Changes in TFP can go hand in hand with increases in measured equality (as seemed to occur in the 1950s) or increases in measured inequality (as in the 1980s). The relation between productivity and welfare will depend on the underlying economic forces shaping productivity growth as well as on public policies toward distribution. Moreover, some of the factors that make productivity difficult to measure may themselves generate welfare gains or losses. Examples include R&D spillovers, the diffusion of innovations, and the temporary market power that provides the incentives for R&D activity. Until we understand these channels of influence better, we must be careful to distinguish productivity growth and welfare improvement.

There is much that remains to be learned about productivity, especially in understanding its economic determinants and its economic and social consequences. The next generations have their work ahead of them. But in the pursuit of this knowledge, we should always remember that we can see farther than our predecessors because we stand on their shoulders.

Notes

References

Credits

Index

NOTES

1. THE DISCOVERY OF THE RESIDUAL

1. This tradition and the databases it developed, together with the development of Keynesian economics, also contributed to the rise of growth theory in the works of Harrod, Domar, and Solow. But that is a different story.

2. The fact that a Dutchman whose country was occupied by the Nazis was publishing in Germany in 1942 caused some comment after the war. This was an example of trying to keep "science" going despite the circumstances—a position that was tenable in 1942 when much of what was happening was not yet widely known.

3. Given the increasing availability of time series data and the general advice of that time to use "de-trended" data, it was not long before trend variables began to appear in production function estimation. The first person to use them, as far as I can tell, was Victor Smith in 1940, in his Northwestern Ph.D. dissertation on the productivity of the steel industry, followed by Tintner in a number of papers based on data for U.S. agriculture (Tintner 1943 and 1946).

4. This was clearly foreshadowed in the earlier exchange between Copeland and Friedman quoted above.

5. There are two major components in Schmookler's dissertation on which this article was based. The primary task of the thesis was the assembly and examination of a consistent series on patenting in the United States, interpreting it as a measure of inventive activity. This part was published in 1954. It is clear that the intent was to bring these two parts together, with the patent series "explaining" the growth in input-over-output series. In a third, unpublished, chapter of his dissertation Schmookler tries to do just that and gets nothing. It is interesting to note that as the result of this outcome he left the productivity measurement field and concentrated on the analysis of patent data, perhaps feeling that they were closer to and a more tangible reflection of the actual processes of invention and innovation that he wanted to study. A generation later I would pursue the same mirage (Griliches 1990).

6. Johnson credits Tintner with stimulating his interest in this approach (personal communication).

2. THE SEARCH FOR EXPLANATIONS

1. Some of the discussion in this and the next section is based on material that appeared earlier in Griliches 1988a, chap. 1, and 1990.

2. Z. Griliches, "Reflections on Reflections . . .," unpublished 1956 manuscript notes in the T. W. Schultz papers at the University of Chicago Library.

3. This formula for technical change holds for any constant returns to scale production function, but the input shares will be constant (independent of factor prices) only for the Cobb-Douglas function.

4. To derive Equation (2.4), first solve (2.2) and (2.3) for the "true" residual measure of technical change, t, which yields: $t = y - f - \alpha (c^\circ - f) - \beta (n^\circ - f) - \gamma z - u$. Subtracting this expression from the conventional measure $\hat{t}$ given in (2.1), and noting (from the definitions of s° and h) that $\alpha = s^\circ(\alpha + \beta) = s^\circ(1 + h)$, we get Equation (2.4) in the text.

5. Measured input shares will be proportional to the output elasticities if the firm minimizes costs (since that requires that the ratio of marginal products equal the factor price ratio) *and* we observe input shares without error.

6. A Tornqvist-Divisia index of aggregate output (input) is simply a weighted average of the rates of growth in its components, where the weights are the revenue shares for each output (cost shares for inputs), which vary over time. The Divisia index allows the weights to vary continuously. The discrete Tornqvist index uses arithmetic average shares between adjacent time periods. Diewert (1976) showed that the Tornqvist-Divisia index is an "exact" index for a wide class of so-called flexible functional forms, and thus it is widely used in empirical work.

7. There is a distant parallel here with the recent burst of work on the new growth economics. The emphasis, particularly in the early part of that literature, on the fact that technical change is endogenous was certainly not news, and there was some exaggeration in claiming this "discovery." The important contribution was to identify the need to introduce imperfect competition in order to explain private innovative activity, and the reciprocal effects of R&D on market structure, and to embed these ideas in an explicit growth model. This line of research has been actively pursued by Aghion and Howitt (1998), and others.

8. Some of the measurement problems are more amenable to correction, such as fixing the bias in price indexes for personal computers and other goods using hedonic methods. But others are conceptually much more difficult, such as valuing gains in life expectancy due to medical technology.

9. Some of it happened in mining and utilities, where output measurement issues are not as severe. Part of the observed decline in productivity in these industries during the 1970s was due to the influence of rising product prices in those sectors, which caused short-run diminishing returns to set in. (See Gordon 1992 for a discussion of one such margin in the electricity generating industry).

10. Hulten (1992) estimates an aggregate production function, adjusting for quality change using the capital goods price indexes developed by Gordon (1990), and concludes that embodied technical change accounts for about 20 percent of output growth in U.S. manufacturing. More recently, Greenwood, Hercowitz, and Krusell (1997) extend the analysis by embedding a vintage capital model into a calibrated (not estimated) general equilibrium framework. Using Gordon's capital price indexes to back out an estimate of the rate of quality improvement, they find that capital embodied technical change accounts for about 60 percent of the (implied balanced) growth in *labor productivity* in the U.S. economy, with "residual" technical change accounting for the remainder. But their model also implies that residual productivity growth regressed sharply since the early 1970s, so the productivity slowdown remains unexplained.

3. THE ROLE OF EDUCATION AND HUMAN CAPITAL

1. This finding was broadly consistent with the earlier finding by Schultz that education accounted for about one fifth of GDP growth, since the residual was computed to be roughly two thirds of GDP growth.

2. See also Hellerstein and Neumark (1998) for a related use of these same data and a "test" based on the direct comparison of wage and marginal product estimates. This line of work has been pursued further in Hellerstein et al. (1996) and in Haegland and Klette (1999), using U.S. and Norwegian data respectively.

3. One might think that this evidence could also be interpreted as a pure signaling story. If equilibrium sorting involves high-ability workers self-selecting into education, then schooling would be correlated with productivity even if education has no real productivity effect. There are two reasons I believe this to be incorrect. First, the "real productivity" hypothesis implies that the output elasticity on schooling should be equal to the elasticity on quality-unadjusted labor, which is confirmed empirically. The signaling interpretation does not generally imply this parameter restriction. The second reason is that the signaling hypothesis implies that the unobservable "ability" should work mainly through its *direct* effect on earnings rather than *via* its effect on the schooling decision. The empirical findings based on factor models using data on siblings, which I discuss in the next section and in note 5 below, do not confirm this prediction.

4. For a more recent analysis of these issues see Kroch and Sjoblom (1994) and Altonji and Pierret (1996).

5. A simple unobservables model that illustrates this finding is:

$$E = \alpha_1 S + \beta_1 A + u_1$$
$$S = \gamma_1 B + \beta_2 A + u_2$$
$$T = \beta_3 A + u_3$$
$$A = \gamma_2 B + f + u_4$$

where E is earnings, S is years of education, T is a preschooling IQ test score, B is a set of background variables (observable individual or family traits), A is unobservable ability, f is the unobserved family effect, and the u's are idiosyncratic errors. The direct effect of ability on earnings is given by the parameter β_1, and the indirect effect, working through the endogenous choice of schooling, is given by β_2. Estimates of such models, and more complicated ones, using sibling data (multiple individuals in each family), typically indicate that $\beta_1 \approx 0$ and $\beta_2 > 0$, as stated in the text.

6. See Willis (1986), Bishop (1992), and Card (1995) for later surveys and for some additional evidence on this topic.

7. For attempts to examine the technology-skill hypothesis, see Huffman (1974), Mincer (1993), Bartel and Lichtenberg (1987), Berman, Bound, and Griliches (1994), and Allen (1996).

8. For examples, see Katz and Murphy (1992), Juhn, Murphy, and Pierce (1993), and Card and Lemieux (1996). Another explanation is that the quality of the less educated has declined relatively because of the increasing number of high school completers. But the shift in the relative numbers is too small and the timing is wrong to explain much of this differential. Also, about two thirds of the widening of the differential has come from a rise in the real wage of the college educated, and only a third from the decline in the real wage of the less educated.

9. See Jovanovic (1997a) for a survey of the role of human capital accumulation in the various versions of "new growth theories."

10. The Israel Central Statistical Bureau Labor Force Surveys, especially nos. 376, 690, and 912, are the source for these numbers.

4. ESTIMATING THE CONTRIBUTION OF R&D

1. Additional surveys can be found in Huffman and Evenson (1993, chap. 7), Mairesse and Sassenou (1991), Alston and Pardey (1996, chap. 6), Hall (1996), Boskin and Lau (1996), and Meijl (1995).

2. To see this, consider a marginal increase in R&D (hence in K), which yields output dY/dK. Suppose that the rents the firm can appropriate from this increment in output decline at constant rate δ and let r be the discount rate. If the firm optimizes, then the present value of the rents must be equal to the marginal cost of R&D: $\int dY/dK e^{-(r+\delta)t} \, dt = 1$, where the integral goes from zero to infinity. This yields $\rho \equiv (r + \delta) = dY/dK$.

3. Pakes and Schankerman (1984) provide one of the first estimates of the depreciation in the value of innovative *output* (as measured by patents). Independent estimates of the depreciation of R&D input are attempted in Nadiri and Prucha (1996) and of physical capital in Pakes and Griliches (1984).

4. The renewal theorem says that the sequence of replacement rates (capital retirement, in our case) tends to a constant value for almost any arbitrary mortality distribution. This theorem is used to justify the geometric decay assumption as an approximation to a broader class of mortality distributions.

5. To derive this equation (4.5), substitute for u_{it} in the expression for y_{it} to get: $y_{it} = \beta x_{it} + \delta k_{it} + \alpha_i + \rho u_{it-1} - e_{it}$. But from Equation (4.3), $u_{it-1} = y_{it-1} - \beta x_{it-1} - \delta k_{it-1} - \alpha_i$. Substituting this into the preceding equation and rearranging terms yields Equation (4.5) in the text.

6. This assumption is right for "stationary" α's, where their effect on y is unchanged over time.

7. The estimation is done by using the Chamberlain (1984) Π-matrix methodology.

8. The distinction is important, because if the firm effect is in fact correlated with the other independent variables, then the estimates using the random effects specification are inconsistent.

9. Generalized method of moments is a general minimum distance estimator that allows us to exploit the fact, in panel data, that the number of valid instruments (appropriately lagged values of variables) differs for each year in which a cross-section sample is available. This makes it possible to use more instruments for some equations than would be the case if we used three-stage least squares, with the same number of instruments in each equation (i.e., each available cross-section).

10. This is equivalent to the Dorfman-Steiner (1954) result for advertising.

11. This form assumes that R&D capital shifts demand but does not affect the price elasticity of demand. A more complex model might also include an interaction term, making the price elasticity itself a function of k.

12. For estimation purposes and to reduce heteroscedasticity, this equation is rewritten in the form $\log (V/A) = \log q + \log (1 + \lambda K/A)$, where $\lambda = b/q$ represents the stock market "premium" to investment in knowledge capital. The estimates in Figure 4.2 are based on unpublished work by B. H. Hall and D. Kim. Alternative computations using balanced panels, robust estimation techniques (e.g., least absolute differences), and industry dummy variables change the absolute magnitude of these coefficients but not the time pattern of the decline in the R&D capital coefficients.

13. The fact that one can interpret γ as representing technological opportunities in the steady state (see Klenow 1996 and Kortum 1996) does not make it a less interesting parameter. One still needs to invest in R&D to take advantage of these opportunities.

14. Two points should be noted. First, the estimate in the text is also an underestimate of the "true" rate of return, because I am using a gross rather than a net measure of R&D investment, leaving out a term proportional to $- \delta K$, where K is the stock of accumulated R&D and δ is its depreciation rate. See Harhoff (1994) for recent evi-

dence on the direction and magnitude of such a bias. Second, to a first approximation, the excess returns bias due to double counting disappears in growth rates. For technical discussion, see Schankerman (1981).

15. Weighting the decline in R&D capital by the coefficient from the first differences regression in Table 4.6, we account for about 40 percent of the slowdown. The figure rises to 55 percent if we use the regression in levels.

5. R&D AND THE PRODUCTIVITY SLOWDOWN

1. This is a view that goes back at least to Knight (1933) and Schultz (1990) and was articulated most recently by Harberger (1990).

2. Among the work done by me and some of my students and associates, see Evenson (1968), Griliches (1973, 1980a, and 1986b), Griliches and Lichtenberg (1984a and 1984b), Griliches and Mairesse (1983 and 1984), Hall (1993), Jaffe (1986), Pakes and Schankerman (1984), Pakes (1986), and Schankerman and Pakes (1986). Important work was also done by other applied researchers, especially Mansfield (1965, 1980, and 1984), Minasian (1962b), Levin et al. (1987), Scherer (1965 and 1982), and Terleckyj (1958 and 1974).

3. The decompositions of productivity (and its deceleration) in Figure 5.1 and Table 4.7 differ for three main reasons: first, Figure 5.1 decomposes labor productivity, while Table 4.7 refers to multifactor productivity; second, the two decompositions use a somewhat different output elasticity weight for R&D capital; and third, the measured stocks of R&D differ slightly owing to the assumed depreciation rate.

4. The "new" growth theories are more helpful in emphasizing the importance of imperfect competition and the role of spillovers in growth and, perhaps, in informing us about cross-country differences in growth performance.

5. Adjusting for labor quality and for the mix of capital assets using Tornqvist indexes does not affect this characterization of the slowdown. Thus I lean toward dating the slowdown at 1973–74, but a case could be made that it began in the late 1960s.

6. For a more optimistic reading of these same facts, see Jorgenson (1996).

7. A more detailed computation based on unpublished data by the BLS leads to essentially the same conclusions (Edwin Dean, private communication).

8. Kuznets is mute on the aggregate story. Implicitly he allows for continued growth through the appearance of new industries, new "general purpose technologies" in modern language (Bresnahan and Trajtenberg 1995). But he is skeptical, as is implied in the opening quotation. He also provides an implicit warning against taking recent data too seriously as indicators of longer term trends when he observes the slowing down of the growth rate in the yield of corn and interprets it as an exhaustion of technological opportunities in agriculture, just before hybrid corn is beginning its diffusion!

9. If R&D capital is growing, then we have to have a rising level of real R&D spending just to prevent a deceleration in the R&D stock and thus a decline in productivity growth. To see this, take the first-difference of the R&D accumulation equation $\Delta K = R - \delta K$, which shows that deceleration sets in ($\Delta \Delta K < 0$) unless $\Delta R > \delta \Delta K$.

6. REMINDERS FOR TRAVELING THE RESEARCH ROAD AHEAD

1. Wilde referred to "the unspeakable in full pursuit of the uneatable." The paraphrase is Solow's (1997, p. 57).

2. I have said too little in this book about the role of science in generating productivity growth. Saying something quantitative about it is even more difficult. For additional discussion and attempts at assessing the contribution of science see Adams and Griliches (1996), Jaffe (1989), Mansfield (1991), Narin et al. (1997), Science Policy Research Unit (1996), and Stephan (1996).

REFERENCES

Abbott, T., Z. Griliches, and J. A. Hausman. 1998. "Short Run Movements in Productivity: Market Power versus Capacity Utilization." In Z. Griliches, ed., *Practicing Econometrics: Essays in Method and Application*. Cheltenham, Eng.: Elgar.

Abramovitz, M. 1956. "Resource and Output Trends in the U.S. since 1870." *American Economic Review*, 46(2): 5–23.

Abramovitz, M., and P. A. David. 1996. "Technological Change and the Rise of Intangible Investments: The U.S. Economy's Growth-Path in the Twentieth Century." In D. Foray and B. A. Lundvall, eds., *Employment and Growth in the Knowledge-Based Economy*, pp. 35–59 (chap. 1). Paris: OECD.

Adams, J. D., and A. B. Jaffe. 1996. "Bounding the Effects of R&D: An Investigation Using Matched Establishment-Firm Data." NBER Working Paper no. 5544. Cambridge, Mass.: National Bureau of Economic Research.

Adams, J. D., and Z. Griliches. 1996. "Measuring Science: An Exploration." *Proceedings of the National Academy of Sciences*, 93: 12,664–12,670.

Aghion, P., and P. Howitt. 1998. *Endogenous Growth Theory*. Cambridge, Mass.: MIT Press.

Allen, D. S. 1997. "Where Is the Productivity Growth (from the Information Technology Revolution)?" *Review* (Federal Reserve Board of St. Louis), March/April: 15–25.

Allen, S. G. 1996. "Technology and the Wage Structure." NBER Working Paper no. 5534. Cambridge, Mass.: National Bureau of Economic Research.

Alston, J., and P. Pardey. 1996. *Making Science Pay: The Economics of Agricultural R&D Policy*. Washington, D.C.: AEI Press.

Altonji, J., and C. Pierret. 1996. "Employer Learning and the Signaling Value of Education." NBER Working Paper no. 5438. Cambridge, Mass.: National Bureau of Economic Research.

Angrist, J., and A. B. Krueger. 1991. "Does Compulsory School Attendance Affect Schooling and Earnings?" *Quarterly Journal of Economics*, 106: 979–1014.

Arellano, M., and O. Bover. 1995. "Another Look at the Instrumental-Variable Estimation of Error-Components Models." *Journal of Econometrics*, 68: 29–52.

Arndt, H. W. 1964. "The Residual Factor." In U.N. Economic Commission for Europe, ed., *Economic Survey of Europe in 1961, Part II: Some Factors in Economic Growth in Europe in the 1950s,* pp. 1–9. Geneva: United Nations. Reprinted in H. W. Arndt, *50 Years of Development Studies* (Canberra: Australian National University, 1993), pp. 53–59.

Arrow, K. J. 1962. "Economic Welfare and the Allocation of Resources for Invention." In *The Rate and Direction of Inventive Activity: Economic and Social Factors,* pp. 609–625. NBER Special Conference Series, vol. 13. Princeton: Princeton University Press.

Ashenfelter, O., and A. B. Kreuger. 1994. "Estimates of the Economic Returns to Schooling from a New Sample of Twins." *American Economic Review,* 84(5): 1157–1173.

Auerbach, A., K. Hassett, and S. Oliner. 1993. "Reassessing the Social Returns to Equipment Investment." NBER Working Paper no. 4405. Cambridge, Mass.: National Bureau of Economic Research.

Australian Industry Commission. 1995. *Appendices,* vol. 3 of *Research and Development.* Report no. 44, May 15. Canberra: Government Publishing Service.

Bachrach, C., 1990. "Essays on Research and Development and Competitiveness." Ph.D. diss., Massachusetts Institute of Technology.

Baily, M. N. 1996. "Trends in Productivity Growth." In J. Fuhrer and J. S. Little, eds., *Technology and Growth,* pp. 269–278. Conference Series no. 40. Boston: Federal Reserve Bank.

Baily, M., and R. Gordon. 1998. "The Productivity Slowdown, Measurement Issues, and the Explosion of Computer Power." *Brookings Papers on Economic Activity,* 2: 347–420.

Barro, R. 1991. "Economic Growth in a Cross Section of Countries." *Quarterly Journal of Economics,* 106: 407–443.

———— 1996. "Determinants of Economic Growth: A Cross-County Empirical Study." NBER Working Paper no. 5698. Cambridge, Mass.: National Bureau of Economic Research.

Barro, R., and J. W. Lee. 1994. "Losers and Winners in Economic Growth." *Proceedings of the World Bank Annual Conference on Development Economics, 1993:* 267–297.

Barro, R., and X. Sala-i-Martin. 1995. *Economic Growth.* New York: McGraw-Hill.

Bartel, A., and F. Lichtenberg. 1987. "The Comparative Advantage of Educated Workers in Implementing New Technology." *Review of Economics and Statistics,* 6: 140–154.

Barton, G. T., and M. R. Cooper. 1948. "Relation of Agricultural Production to Inputs." *Review of Economics and Statistics,* 30(2): 117–126.

Basant, R., and B. Fikkert. 1996. "The Effects of R&D, Foreign Technology Purchase, and International and Domestic Spillovers on Productivity in Indian Firms." *Review of Economics and Statistics,* 78(2): 187–199.

Basu, S., and J. Fernald. 1995. "Aggregate Productivity and the Productivity of Aggregates." International Finance Discussion Paper no. 532. Washington, D.C.: Board of Governors of the Federal Reserve System.

Basu, S., and M. Kimball. 1997. "Cyclical Productivity with Unobserved Input Variation." NBER Working Paper no. 5915. Cambridge, Mass.: National Bureau of Economic Research.

Becker, G. S. 1962. "Investment in Human Capital: A Theoretical Analysis." *Journal of Political Economy,* 70: 9–49.

Benhabib, J., and B. Jovanovic. 1991. "Externalities and Growth Accounting." *American Economic Review,* 81(1): 82–113.

Benhabib, J., and M. Spiegel. 1991. "Growth Accounting with Physical and Human Capital Accumulation." Economic Research Reports, 91–66. New York: NYU C. V. Star Center.

——— 1994. "The Role of Human Capital in Economic Development: Evidence from Aggregate Cross-Country Data." *Journal of Monetary Economics,* 34: 143–173.

Ben-Porath, Y. 1967. "The Production of Human Capital and the Life Cycle of Earnings." *Journal of Political Economy,* 75: 352–365.

——— ed. 1986. *The Israeli Economy: Maturing through Crises.* Cambridge, Mass.: Harvard University Press.

Berglas, E. 1965. "Investment and Technological Change." *Journal of Political Economy,* 73(2): 173–180.

Berman, E., J. Bound, and Z. Griliches. 1994. "Changes in the Demand for Skilled Labor within U.S. Manufacturing Industries: Evidence from the Annual Survey of Manufacturing." *Quarterly Journal of Economics,* 109: 367–398.

Bernstein, J. I. 1994. *International R&D Spillovers between Industries in Canada and the United States.* Working Paper no. 3. Ottawa: Industry Canada.

——— 1997. "Interindustry R&D Spillovers for Electrical and Electronic Products: The Canadian Case." *Economic Systems Research,* 9(1): 111–125.

Bishop, J. 1992. "The Impact of Academic Competencies on Wages, Unemployment, and Job Performance." *Carnegie-Rochester Conference Series on Public Policy,* 37: 127–194. Amsterdam: North-Holland.

Blinder, A., and Y. Weiss. 1976. "Human Capital and Labor Supply: A Synthesis." *Journal of Political Economy,* 84: 449–472.

Blundell, R., and S. Bond. 1996. "GMM Estimation with Highly Persistent Panel Data:

An Application to Production Function Estimation." Manuscript, University College, London.

Bosca, J., A. de la Fuenta, and R. Domenech. 1996. "Human Capital and Growth: Theory Ahead of Measurement?" Unpublished paper, Universidad Autonoma de Barcelona, Barcelona.

Boskin, M., and L. Lau. 1996. "Contributions of R&D to Economic Growth." In B. Smith and C. Barfield, eds., *Technology, R&D, and the Economy,* pp. 75–113. Washington: Brookings and AEI Press.

Bresnahan, T., and M. Trajtenberg. 1995. "General Purpose Technologies: 'Engines of Growth?'" *Journal of Econometrics,* 65(1): 83–108.

Brouwer, E., and A. Kleinknecht. 1997. "Measuring the Unmeasurable: A Country's Non-R&D Expenditure on Product and Service Innovation." *Research Policy,* 25: 1235–1242.

Brozen, Y. 1960. "Trends in Industrial Research and Development." *Journal of Business,* 33(3): 204–217.

BLS. 1983. *Trends in Multifactor Productivity, 1948–81.* Bulletin no. 2178. Washington, D.C.: U.S. Department of Labor.

——— 1993. *Labor Composition and U.S. Productivity Growth, 1948–90.* Bulletin no. 2426, December. Washington, D.C.: U.S. Department of Labor.

——— 1999. *Multifactor Productivity Trends, 1997.* Washington, D.C.: U.S. Department of Labor.

——— Periodically. *Multifactor Productivity Trends.* Washington, D.C.: U.S. Department of Labor.

Burnside, C. 1996. "Industry Innovation: Where and Why, A Comment." *Carnegie-Rochester Conference Series on Public Policy,* 44:151–167.

Caballero, R. A., and A. Jaffe. 1993. "How High Are the Giants' Shoulders." *NBER Macroeconomics Annual, 1993.* Cambridge, Mass.: MIT. Press.

Cameron, G. 1996. "Innovation and Growth." D.Phil. thesis, Nuffeld College, Oxford.

Card, D. 1995. "Earnings, Schooling, and Ability Revisited." *Research in Labor Economics,* 14: 23–48.

——— 1999. "The Causal Effect of Education on Earnings." In O. Ashenfelter and D. Card, eds., *Handbook of Labor Economics,* vol. 3A, pp. 1801–1863. Amsterdam: Elsevier.

Card, D., and T. Lemieux. 1996. "Wage Dispersion, Returns to Skill, and Black-White Wage Differentials." *Journal of Econometrics,* 74: 319–361.

Carson, C. S. 1975. "The History of the U.S. National Income and Products Accounts:

The Development of an Analytical Tool." *Review of Income and Wealth,* 21(2): 153–182.

Central Bureau of Statistics. 1970, 1980, 1990. Labor Force Surveys, Special Series nos. 376, 690, and 912. Jerusalem, Israel.

Chamberlain, G. 1984. "Panel Data." In Z. Griliches and M. Intriligator, eds., *Handbook of Econometrics,* vol. 2, pp. 1247–1318. Amsterdam: North-Holland.

Chinloy, P. T. 1980. "Sources of Quality Change in Labor Input." *American Economic Review,* 70(1): 108–119.

Cockburn, I., and Z. Griliches. 1988. "Industry Effects and Appropriability Measures in the Stock Market's Valuation of R&D and Patents." *American Economic Review Papers and Proceedings,* 78(2): 419–423.

Cockburn, I., and R. Henderson. 1997. "Public-Private Interaction and the Productivity of Pharmaceutical Research." NBER Working Paper no. 6018. Cambridge, Mass.: National Bureau of Economic Research.

Coe, D. T., and E. Helpman. 1995. "International R&D Spillovers." *European Economic Review,* 39: 859–887.

Coe, D., E. Helpman, and A. Hoffmeister. 1997. "North-South Spillovers." *Economic Journal,* 107(440): 134–149.

Copeland, M. A. 1937. "Concepts of National Income." In *Studies in Income and Wealth,* vol. 1, pp. 3–63. New York: National Bureau of Economic Research.

Copeland, M. A., and E. M. Martin. 1938. "The Correction of Wealth and Income Estimates for Price Changes." In *Studies in Income and Wealth,* vol. 2, pp. 85–135 (includes discussion by M. Friedman). New York: National Bureau of Economic Research.

Corrado, C., and L. Slifman. 1999. "Decomposition of Productivity and Unit Costs." *American Economic Review,* 89(2): 328–332.

Crepon, B., E. Duguet, and J. Mairesse. 1998. "Research, Innovation, and Productivity: An Econometric Analysis at the Firm Level." *Economics of Innovation and New Technology,* 7(2): 115–158.

David, P. 1966. "The Mechanization of Reaping in the Antebellum Midwest." In H. Rosovsky, ed., *Industrialization in Two Systems: Essays in Honor of Alexander Gerschenkron,* pp. 3–28. New York: Wiley.

——— 1991. "Computer and Dynamo: The Modern Productivity Paradox in a Not-Too-Distant Mirror." In *Technology and Productivity,* pp. 315–348. Paris: OECD.

De Long, J. B. 1996. "Cross-Country Variations in National Economic Growth Rates: The Role of 'Technology.'" In J. Fuhrer and J. S. Little, eds., *Technology and*

Growth, pp. 127–150 (with discussions by J. Frankel, pp. 151–166, and A. Jaffe, pp. 167–172). Conference Series no. 40. Boston: Federal Reserve Bank.

De Long, J. B., and L. Summers. 1991. "Equipment Investment and Economic Growth." *Quarterly Journal of Economics,* 106(2): 445–502.

Denison, E. F. 1962. *The Sources of Economic Growth in the U.S. and the Alternatives before Us.* Supplementary Paper no. 13. New York: Committee for Economic Development.

———— 1964a. "Measuring the Contribution of Education." In *The Residual Factor and Economic Growth,* pp. 13–55, 77–102. Paris: OECD.

———— 1964b. "The Unimportance of the Embodiment Question." *American Economic Review,* 54(March): 90–94.

———— 1969. "Some Major Issues in Productivity Analysis: An Examination of Estimates by Jorgenson and Griliches." *Survey of Current Business,* 49(5, part 2): 1–27.

———— 1974. *Accounting for United States Economic Growth, 1929–1969.* Washington, D.C.: Brookings Institution.

———— 1979. *Accounting for Slower Economic Growth.* Washington, D.C.: Brookings Institution.

———— 1984. "Accounting for Slower Economic Growth: An Update." In J. W. Kendrick, ed., *International Comparisons of Productivity and Causes of the Slowdown,* pp. 1–46. Cambridge, Mass.: Ballinger.

———— 1985. *Trends in American Economic Growth, 1929–1982.* Washington, D.C.: Brookings Institution.

Diewert, W. E. 1976. "Exact and Superlative Index Numbers." *Journal of Econometrics,* 4(2): 115–145.

Diewert, W. E., and K. Fox. 1999. "Can Measurement Error Explain the Productivity Paradox?" *Canadian Journal of Economics,* 32(2): 251–280.

Dorfman, R., and P. O. Steiner. 1954. "Optimal Advertising and Optimal Quality." *American Economic Review,* 44(December): 826–836.

Dougherty, C., and D. W. Jorgenson. 1996. "International Comparisons of the Sources of Economic Growth." *American Economic Review Papers and Proceedings,* 86: 25–29.

Eaton, J., and S. Kortum. 1997. "International Technology Diffusion: Theory and Measurement." Unpublished paper, Boston University.

Eden, B., and Z. Griliches. 1993. "Productivity, Market Power, and Capacity Utilization When Spot Markets Are Complete." *American Economic Association Papers and Proceedings,* 83(2): 219–223.

Ellison, T. 1886. *The Cotton Trade of Great Britain.* London: E. Wilson.

Englander, A. S., and A. Gurney. 1994. "Medium-Term Determinants of OECD Productivity." *OECD Economic Studies,* 22(Spring): 49–109.

Evenson, R. E. 1968. "The Contribution of Agricultural Research and Extension to Agricultural Productivity." Ph.D. diss., University of Chicago.

——— 1984. "International Invention: Implications for Technology Market Analysis." In Z. Griliches, ed., *R&D, Patents, and Productivity,* pp. 89–123. Chicago: University of Chicago Press.

——— 1996. "Two Blades of Grass: Research for U.S. Agriculture." In J. M. Antle and D. A. Sumner, eds., *The Economics of Agriculture: Papers in Honor of D. Gale Johnson,* vol. 2, pp. 71–203. Chicago: University of Chicago Press.

——— 1997. "Industrial Productivity Growth Linkages between OECD Countries, 1970–90." *Economic Systems Research,* 9(2): 221–230.

Fabricant, S. 1954. *Economic Progress and Economic Change.* New York: National Bureau of Economic Research.

Freeman, R. B. 1976. *The Overeducated American.* New York: Academic Press.

Frankel, J., and D. Romer. 1996. "Trade and Growth: An Empirical Investigation." NBER Working Paper no. 5476. Cambridge, Mass.: National Bureau of Economic Research.

Frantzen, D. 1997. "Innovation-Driven Growth and International R&D Spillovers." Unpublished paper, Free University of Brussels.

Friedman, M. 1938. "Comment." In *Studies in Income and Wealth,* vol. 2, pp. 123–130. New York: National Bureau of Economic Research.

Friedman, M., and S. Kuznets. 1945. *Income from Independent Professional Practice.* New York: National Bureau of Economic Research.

Goldberger, A., and C. Manski. 1995. *"The Bell Curve:* Review Article." *Journal of Economic Literature,* 33: 762–776.

Gordon, R. J. 1968. "The Disappearance of Productivity Change." Economic Development Paper 105. Harvard University.

——— 1992. "Forward into the Past: Productivity Retrogression in the Electric Generating Industry." NBER Working Paper no. 3988. Cambridge, Mass.: National Bureau of Economic Research.

——— 1996. "Problems in the Measurement and Performance of Service-Sector Productivity in the United States." NBER Working Paper no. 5519. Cambridge, Mass.: National Bureau of Economic Research.

——— 1998. *Macroeconomics,* 7th ed. Reading, Mass.: Addison-Wesley-Longman.

———— 1999. "U.S. Economic Growth since 1870: One Big Wave?" *American Economic Review Papers and Proceedings,* 89(2): 123–128.

———— 2000. "Current Productivity Puzzles from a Long-Term Perspective." In B. van Ark, S. Kuipers, and G. Kuper, eds., *Productivity, Technology, and Economic Growth.* Norwell, Mass.: Kluwer.

Gordon, R., M. Schankerman, and R. Spady. 1986. "Estimating the Effects of R&D on Bell System Productivity: A Model of Embodied Technical Change." In M. Preston and R. Quandt, eds., *Prices, Competition, and Equilibrium,* pp. 164–190. Oxford: Philip Allan Press.

Greenwood, J., Z. Hercowitz, and P. Krussel. 1997. "Long-Run Implications of Investment-Specific Technological Change." *American Economic Review,* 87(3): 342–362.

Greenwood, J., and M. Yorukoglu. 1997. "1974." *Carnegie-Rochester Conference Series on Public Policy,* 46(June): 49–95.

Griliches, Z. 1957. "Hybrid Corn: An Exploration in the Economics of Technological Change." *Econometrica,* 25(4): 501–522.

———— 1958. "Research Cost and Social Returns: Hybrid Corn and Related Innovations." *Journal of Political Economy,* 66(5): 419–431.

———— 1960a. "Measuring Inputs in Agriculture: A Critical Survey." *Journal of Farm Economics,* 42(5): 1411–1433.

———— 1960b. "Hybrid Corn and the Economics of Innovation." *Science,* 132(July 29): 275–280.

———— 1961. "Hedonic Price Indexes for Automobiles: An Econometric Analysis of Quality Change." In *The Price Statistics of the Federal Government.* General Series, no. 73. New York: National Bureau of Economic Research.

———— 1963a. "The Sources of Measured Productivity Growth: U.S. Agriculture, 1940–1960." *Journal of Political Economy,* 81(4): 331–346.

———— 1963b. "Capital Stock in Investment Functions: Some Problems of Concept and Measurement." In C. F. Christ et al., eds., *Measurement in Economics: Studies in Mathematical Economics and Econometrics in Memory of Yehuda Grunfeld,* pp. 115–137. Stanford: Stanford University Press.

———— 1963c. "Production Functions, Technical Change, and All That." Report 6328, Econometric Institute, Netherlands School of Economics. Rotterdam.

———— 1964. "Research Expenditures, Education, and the Aggregate Agricultural Production Function." *American Economic Review,* 54(6): 961–974.

———— 1967. "Production Functions in Manufacturing: Some Preliminary Results." In M. Brown, ed. *The Theory and Empirical Analysis of Production,* pp. 275–

340. NBER Studies in Income and Wealth, vol. 31. New York: Columbia University Press.

——— 1969. "Capital Skill Complementarity." *Review of Economics and Statistics,* 51: 465–468.

——— 1970. "Notes on the Role of Education in Production Functions and Growth Accounting." In L. Hansen, ed., *Education, Income, and Human Capital,* pp. 71–115. NBER Studies in Income and Wealth, vol. 35. New York: Columbia University Press.

——— 1973. "Research Expenditures and Growth Accounting." In B. R. Williams, ed., *Science and Technology in Economic Growth,* pp. 59–95. London: MacMillan.

——— 1977. "Estimating the Returns to Schooling: Some Econometric Problems." *Econometrica,* 45(1): 1–22.

——— 1979. "Sibling Models and Data in Economics: Beginnings of a Survey." *Journal of Political Economy,* 87(5, part 2): S37–S64.

——— 1980a. "R&D and the Productivity Slowdown." *American Economic Review Papers and Proceedings,* 70(2): 343–348.

——— 1980b. "Returns to Research and Development Expenditures in the Private Sector." In J. W. Kendrick and B. Vaccara, eds., *New Developments in Productivity Measurement,* pp. 419–454. NBER Studies in Income and Wealth, vol. 44. Chicago: Chicago University Press.

——— 1981. "Market Value, R&D, and Patents." *Economics Letters,* 7: 83–187.

——— 1986a. "Economic Data Issues." In Z. Griliches and M. Intriligator, eds., *Handbook of Econometrics,* pp. 1466–1514. Amsterdam: North-Holland.

——— 1986b. "Productivity, R&D, and Basic Research at the Firm Level in the 1970s." *American Economic Review,* 76(1): 141–154.

——— 1988a. *Technology, Education, and Productivity: Early Papers with Notes to Subsequent Literature.* New York: Basil Blackwell.

——— 1988b. "Productivity Puzzles and R&D: Another Nonexplanation." *The Journal of Economic Perspectives,* 2(4): 9–21.

——— 1990. "Patent Statistics as Economic Indicators: A Survey." *Journal of Economic Literature,* 28(4): 1661–1707.

——— 1992a. "The Search for R&D Spillovers." *The Scandinavian Journal of Economics,* 94: 29–47.

——— ed. 1992b. "Introduction." In Z. Griliches, ed., *Output Measurement in the Service Sectors,* pp. 1–22. NBER Studies in Income and Wealth, vol. 56. Chicago: University of Chicago Press.

—— 1994. "Productivity, R&D, and the Data Constraint." *American Economic Review*, 84: 1–23.

—— 1995. "R&D and Productivity: Econometric Results and Measurement Issues." In P. Stoneman, ed., *Handbook of the Economics of Innovation and Technological Change*, pp. 52–89. Oxford, Eng., and Cambridge, Mass.: Basil Blackwell.

—— 1996. "The Discovery of the Residual: A Historical Note." *Journal of Economic Literature*, 34(Sept.): 1324–1330.

—— 1997. "Education, Human Capital, and Growth: A Personal Perspective." *Journal of Labor Economics*, 15(1, part 2): S330–S344.

—— 1998a. "R&D and Productivity: The Unfinished Business." In Griliches, *R&D and Productivity: The Econometric Evidence*. Chicago: University of Chicago Press.

—— 1998b. *R&D and Productivity: The Econometric Evidence*. Chicago: University of Chicago Press.

Griliches, Z., and D. W. Jorgenson. 1966. "Sources of Measured Productivity Change: Capital Input." *American Economic Review*, 56(2): 50–61.

Griliches Z., and F. Lichtenberg. 1984a. "R&D and Productivity Growth at the Industry Level: Is There Still a Relationship?" In Z. Griliches, ed., *R&D, Patents, and Productivity*, pp. 465–496. Chicago: University of Chicago Press.

—— 1984b. "Interindustry Technology Flows and Productivity Growth: A Reexamination." *The Review of Economics and Statistics*, 66(2): 324–329.

Griliches, Z., and J. Mairesse. 1983. "Comparing Productivity Growth: An Exploration of French and U.S. Industrial and Firm Data." *European Economic Review*, 21: 89–119.

—— 1984. "Productivity and R&D at the Firm Level." In Z. Griliches, ed., *R&D, Patents, and Productivity*, pp. 339–374. Chicago: University of Chicago Press.

—— 1998. "Production Functions: The Search for Identification." In Z. Griliches, *Practicing Econometrics: Essays in Method and Application*, pp. 383–411. Cheltenham, Eng.: Edward Elgar. Reprinted in S. Strom, ed., *Econometrics and Economic Theory in the Twentieth Century: The Ragnar Frisch Centennial Symposium*, pp. 169–203. Cambridge: Cambridge University Press.

Griliches, Z., and W. Mason. 1972. "Education, Income, and Ability." *Journal of Political Economy*, 80(3, part 2): 285–316.

Griliches, Z., and H. Regev. 1995. "Firm Productivity in Israeli Industry, 1979–1988." *Journal of Econometrics*, 65: 175–203.

Griliches, Z., and V. Ringstad. 1971. *Economies of Scale and the Form of the Production Function*. Amsterdam: North-Holland.

Grossman, G., and E. Helpman. 1991. "Quality Ladders in the Theory of Growth." *Review of Economic Studies,* 58: 43–61.

Grupp, H. 1966. "Spillover Effects and the Science Base of Innovations Reconsidered: An Empirical Approach." *Evolutionary Economics,* 6(2): 175–197.

Gullickson, W. 1995. "Measurement of Productivity Growth in U.S. Manufacturing." *Monthly Labor Review,* 118(7): 13–28.

Haegeland, T., and T. J. Klette. 1999. "Do Higher Wages Reflect Higher Productivity?: Education, Gender, and Experience Premiums in a Matched Plant-Worker Data Set." In J. Haltiwanger, J. Lane, J. R. Spletzer, J. Theeuwes, and K. Troske, eds., *The Creation and Analysis of Employer-Employee Matched Data.* Amsterdam: North-Holland.

Hall, B. H. 1993. "Industrial Research in the 1980s: Did the Rate of Return Fall?" *Brookings Papers on Economic Activity: Microeconomics,* 2: 289–331.

——— 1996. "The Private and Social Returns to Research and Development." In B. Smith and C. Barfield, eds., *Technology, R&D, and the Economy,* pp. 140–162. Washington, D.C.: Brookings Institution and AEI.

Hall, B. H., and F. Hayashi. 1989. "Research and Development as an Investment." University of California at Berkeley, Working Paper in Economics, 89–108.

Hall, B. H., and D. Kim. 1999. "Valuing Intangible Assets: The Stock Market Value of R&D Revisited." Manuscript, University of California at Berkeley.

Hall, R. E. 1988. "The Relation between Price and Marginal Cost in U.S. Industry." *Journal of Political Economy,* 96(5): 921–947.

Hanel, P. 1994. "R&D, Inter-Industry, and International Spillovers of Technology and the Total Factor Productivity Growth of Manufacturing Industries in Canada, 1974–89." Working Paper no. 94-04. Quebec: University of Sherbrooke.

Harberger, A. 1990. "The Sources of Growth Revisited." Presidential address at the 1990 meetings of the Western Economic Association.

Harhoff, D. 1994. "R&D and Productivity in German Manufacturing Firms." ZEW Discussion Paper no. 94-01. Mannheim: Zentrum für Europäische Wirtschaftsforschung.

——— 1995. "The Effect of Knowledge Externalities and Technological Proximity on R&D Spending and Productivity." Unpublished paper. Mannheim: ZEW.

Hayek, F. A. 1945. "The Use of Knowledge in Society." *American Economic Review,* 35(4): 519–530.

Heady, E. O., and J. L. Dillon. 1961. *Agricultural Production Functions.* Ames: Iowa State University Press.

Heckman, J. J. 1976. "A Life-Cycle Model of Earnings, Learning, and Consumption." *Journal of Political Economy,* 84: S11–S44.

Heckman, J. J., and T. E. MaCurdy. 1980. "A Life Cycle Model of Female Labour Supply." *The Review of Economic Studies,* 47: 47–74.

Hellerstein, J. K., and D. Neumark. 1998. "Sex, Wages, and Productivity: An Empirical Analysis of Israeli Firm-Level Data." *Industrial Relations,* 37(2): 232–260.

Hellerstein, J. K., D. Neumark, and K. Troske. 1996. "Wages, Productivity, and Worker Characteristics: Evidence from Plant-Level Production Functions and Wage Equations." NBER Working Paper no. W5626. Cambridge, Mass.: National Bureau of Economic Research.

Herrnstein, R. J., and C. Murray. 1994. *The Bell Curve: Intelligence and Class Structure in American Life.* New York: Free Press.

Hicks, J. R. 1940. "The Valuation of the Social Income." *Economica,* 7(May): 105–124.

Hornstein, A., and P. Krussel. 1996. "Can Technology Improvements Cause Productivity Slowdowns." In *NBER Macroeconomics Annual,* pp. 209–225. Cambridge, Mass.: MIT Press.

Houthakker, H. S. 1959. "Education and Income." *Review of Economics and Statistics,* 41: 24–28.

Howitt, P. 1998. "Measurement, Obsolescence, and General Purpose Technologies." In E. Helpman, ed., *General Purpose Technologies and Economic Growth.* Cambridge, Mass.: MIT Press.

Huffman, W. E. 1974. "Decision Making: The Role of Education." *American Journal of Agricultural Economics,* 56: 85–97.

Huffman, W. E., and R. Evenson. 1993. *Science for Agriculture.* Ames: Iowa State University Press.

Hulten, C. 1992. "Growth Accounting When Technical Change Is Embodied in Capital." *American Economic Review,* 82(4): 964–980.

Inkmann, J., and W. Pohlmeier. 1995. "R&D Spillovers, Technological Distance, and Innovative Success." Manuscript, University of Constance.

Jaffe, A. 1986. "Technological Opportunity and Spillovers of R&D: Evidence from Firms' Patents, Profits, and Market Value." *American Economic Review,* 75(6): 984–1002.

——— 1989. "Real Effects of Academic Research." *The American Economic Review,* 79(5): 957–970.

Jaffe, A., and M. Trajtenberg. 1999. "International Knowledge Flows: Evidence from Patent Citations." *Economics of Innovation & New Technology,* 8(1–2): 105–136.

Jamison, D. T., and L. J. Lau. 1982. *Farm Education and Farm Efficiency.* Baltimore: Johns Hopkins University Press.

Jefferson, G. 1997. "The Tyranny of Growth Accounting: An Analytical Perspective on Growth in E. Asia (and Elsewhere)." Manuscript, Brandeis University.

Jevons, W. S. 1866. *The Coal Question: An Inquiry concerning the Progress of the Nation and the Probable Exhaustion of Our Coal-Mines,* 2nd ed. London: Macmillan.

Johnson, D. G. 1950. "The Nature of the Supply Function for Agricultural Products." *American Economic Review,* 40(4): 539–564.

Jones, C. 1994. "Economic Growth and the Relative Price of Capital." *Journal of Monetary Economics,* 34 (December): 359–382.

——— 1995. "R&D-Based Models of Economic Growth." *Journal of Political Economy,* 103(4): 759–784.

——— 1997. "The Upcoming Slowdown in U.S. Economic Growth." Manuscript, Stanford University.

Jorgenson, D. W. 1966. "The Embodiment Hypothesis." *Journal of Political Economy,* 74: 1–77.

——— 1974. "The Economic Theory of Replacement and Depreciation." In W. Sellekaerts, ed., *Econometrics and Economic Theory,* pp. 189–221. New York: Macmillan.

——— 1990. "Productivity and Economic Growth." In E. R. Berndt and J. E. Triplett, eds., *Fifty Years of Economic Measurement,* pp. 19–118. NBER Studies in Income and Wealth, vol. 34. Chicago: University of Chicago Press.

——— 1996. "Technology in Growth Theory." In J. Fuhrer and J. S. Little, eds., *Technology and Growth,* pp. 45–77 (with discussions by S. Basu, pp. 78–82, and G. Grossman, pp. 83–89). Conference Series no. 40. Boston: Federal Reserve Bank.

Jorgenson, D. W., and B. Fraumeni. 1992a. "Investment in Education and U.S. Economic Growth." *Scandinavian Journal of Economics,* 94: S51–S70.

——— 1992b. "The Output of the Education Sector." In Z. Griliches, ed., *Output Measurement in the Service Sectors,* pp. 303–338. NBER Studies in Income and Wealth, vol. 56. Chicago: University of Chicago Press.

Jorgenson, D. W., and F. M. Gollop. 1992. "Productivity Growth in U.S. Agriculture: A Postwar Perspective." *American Journal of Agricultural Economics,* 74(3): 745–750. Reprinted in D. W. Jorgenson, ed., *Productivity: Postwar U.S. Economic Growth* (Cambridge, Mass.: MIT Press, 1995), pp. 389–400.

Jorgenson, D. W., F. M. Gollop, and B. M. Fraumeni. 1987. *Productivity and U.S. Economic Growth.* Cambridge, Mass.: Harvard University Press.

Jorgenson, D. W., and Z. Griliches. 1967. "The Explanation of Productivity Change." *Review of Economic Studies,* 34(3): 249–283.

———— 1972. "Issues in Growth Accounting: A Reply to Edward F. Denison, and Final Reply." *Survey of Current Business*, 52(5, part 2): 31–111. (Special issue entitled *The Measurement of Productivity*).

Jorgenson, D. W., and A. Pachon. 1982. "The Accumulation of Human and Non-Human Capital." In R. Hemming and F. Modigliani, eds., *The Determinants of National Saving and Wealth*, pp. 302–350. London: MacMillan.

Jorgenson, D. W., M. S. Ho, and B. M. Fraumeni. 1994. "Quality of the U.S. Work Force, 1948–90." Manuscript, Harvard University.

Jorgenson, D. W., and E. Yip. 2000. "Whatever Happened to Productivity Growth?: Investment and Growth in the G7." In E. R. Dean, M. J. Harper, and C. Hulten, eds., *New Developments in Productivity Analysis*. Chicago: University of Chicago Press.

Jovanovic, B. 1997a. "Learning and Growth." In D. Kreps and K. Wallis, eds., *Advances in Economics*, vol. 2, pp 318–339. Cambridge: Cambridge University Press.

———— "Obsolescence of Capital." 1997b. Manuscript, New York University.

Jovanovic, B., S. Lach, and V. Lavy. 1993. "Growth and the Cost Reducing Role of Human Capital." Working Paper (May), New York University.

Judson, R. 1996. "Do Low Human Capital Coefficients Make Sense? A Puzzle and Some Answers." Finance and Economics Discussion Series no. 96-13, March. Washington, D.C.: Federal Reserve Board.

Juhn, C., K. M. Murphy, and B. Pierce. 1993. "Wage Inequality and the Returns to Skill." *Journal of Political Economy*, 101: 410–442.

Katz, L., and K. M. Murphy. 1992. "Changes in the Wage Structure, 1963–87: Supply and Demand Factors." *Quarterly Journal of Economics*, 107: 35–78.

Keller, W. 1997. "Trade and the Transmission of Technology." NBER Working Paper 6113. Cambridge, Mass.: National Bureau of Economic Research.

Kendrick, J. W. 1995. "Productivity." In S. Fabricant, ed., *Government in Economic Life*, 35th Annual Report, pp. 44–47. New York: National Bureau of Economic Research.

———— 1956. *Productivity Trends: Capital and Labor.* New York: National Bureau of Economic Research.

———— 1961. *Productivity Trends in the U.S.* Princeton: Princeton University Press.

———— 1983. "International Comparisons of Recent Productivity Trends." In S. H. Shurr, S. Sonenblum, and D. Wood, eds., *Energy, Productivity, and Economic Growth.* Cambridge, Mass.: Oelgeschlager, Gunn, and Hain.

Klenow, P. 1996. "Industry Innovation: Where and Why." *Carnegie-Rochester Conference Series on Public Policy*, 44: 125–150.

———— 1998. "Ideas versus Rival Human Capital: Industry Evidence on Growth Models." *Journal of Monetary Economics,* 42(1): 3–23.

Klette, T. J. 1996. "R&D, Scope Economies, and Plant Performance." *RAND Journal of Economics,* 27(3): 502–522.

Klette, T. J., and Z. Griliches. 1996. "The Inconsistency of Common Scale Estimators When Output Prices Are Unobserved and Endogenous." *Journal of Applied Econometrics,* 11: 343–361.

Klette, T. J., and F. Johansen. 1996. "Accumulation of R&D Capital and Dynamic Firm Performance: A Not-So-Fixed Effect Model." Discussion Paper no. 184, November. Oslo: Statistics Norway.

Klinov, R. 1986. "Changes in the Industrial Structure." In Y. Ben-Porath, ed., *The Israeli Economy: Maturing through Crisis,* pp. 119–136. Cambridge, Mass.: Harvard University Press.

Knight, F. H. 1933. *Risk, Uncertainty, and Profit,* 2nd. ed. London.

Kortum, S. 1996. "Discussion" of E. Mansfield's "Microeconomic Policy and Technological Change." In J. Fuhrer and J. S. Little, eds., *Technology and Growth,* pp. 200–207. Conference Series no. 40. Boston: Federal Reserve Bank.

Kortum, S., and S. Lach. 1955. "Patents and Productivity Growth in U.S. Manufacturing Industries." Manuscript, Boston University.

Kortum, S., and J. Lerner. 1998. "Stronger Protection or Technological Revolution: What Is behind the Recent Surge in Patenting?" *Carnegie-Rochester Conference Series on Public Policy,* 48(0): 247–304.

Kroch, E. A., and K. Sjoblom. 1994. "Schooling as Human Capital or a Signal." *Journal of Human Resources,* 29: 156–180.

Kuznets, S. S. 1930. *Secular Movements in Production and Prices.* Boston: Houghton Mifflin.

Kyriacou, G. A. 1991. "Level and Growth Effects of Human Capital." C. V. Star Center Economic Research Reports. New York: New York University.

Lach, S., 1994. "Non-Rivalry of Knowledge and R&D's Contribution to Productivity." Working Paper no. 289, June. Jerusalem: Hebrew University.

Landes, D. *The Unbound Prometheus.* Cambridge: Cambridge University Press.

Levin, R., A. Klevorick, R. Nelson, and S. Winter. 1987. "Appropriating the Returns from Industrial Research and Development." *Brookings Papers on Economic Activity,* 3: 783–820.

Los, B., and B. Verspagen. 1996. "R&D Spillovers and Productivity: Evidence from U.S. Manufacturing Microdata." MERIT 2/96–007. Maastricht Economic Research Institute on Innovation and Technology, Maastricht University, Netherlands.

Lucas, R. E. 1988. "On the Mechanics of Economic Development." *Journal of Monetary Economics*, 22: 3–42.

———— 1993. "Making a Miracle." *Econometrica*, 61(2): 251–272.

Lysko, W. 1995. "Manufacturing Multifactor Productivity in Three Countries." U.S. Department of Labor, *Monthly Labor Review* (U.S. Department of Labor), July: 39–55.

Mairesse, J., and Z. Griliches. 1990. "Heterogeneity in Panel Data: Are There Stable Production Functions?" In P. Champsaur et al., eds., *Essays in Honor of Edmond Malinvaud*, vol. 3, pp. 193–231. Cambridge, Mass.: MIT Press.

Mairesse, J., and B. H. Hall. 1996. "Estimating the Productivity of Research and Development in French and U.S. Manufacturing Firms: An Exploration of Simultaneity Issues with GMM Methods." In K. Wagner and B. Van Ark, eds., *International Productivity Differences and Their Explanations*, pp. 285–315. Amsterdam: Elsevier Science.

Mairesse, J., and P. Mohnen. 1994. "R&D and Productivity Growth: What Have We Learned from Econometric Studies?" In *Proceedings of the EUNETIC (European Network on the Economics of Technological and Institutional Change) Conference on Evolutionary Economics of Technological Change: Assessment of Results and New Frontiers*, pp. 817–888. Strasbourg: BETA, Strasbourg Communaute Urbaine.

Mairesse, J., and M. Sassenou. 1991. "R&D and Productivity: A Survey of Econometric Studies at the Firm Level." *Science-Technology Industry Review*, 8: 9–43.

Mankiw. G. 1995. "The Growth of Nations." *Brookings Papers on Economic Activity*, 1: 275–310, 324–326.

Mankiw. N. G., D. Romer, and D. N. Weil. 1992. "A Contribution to the Empirics of Economic Growth." *Quarterly Journal of Economics*, 107(2): 407–437.

Mansfield. E. 1961. "Technical Change and the Rate of Imitation." *Econometrica*, 29: 741–766.

———— 1965. "Rates of Return from Industrial R&D." *American Economic Review*, 55: 310–322.

———— 1980. "Basic Research and Productivity Increase in Manufacturing." *American Economic Review*, 70: 863–873.

———— 1984. "R&D and Innovation: Some Empirical Findings." In Z. Griliches, ed., *R&D, Patents, and Productivity*, pp. 127–154. Chicago: University of Chicago Press.

———— 1991. "Academic Research and Industrial Innovation." *Research Policy*, 20: 1–12.

Manski, C. 1993. "Identification of Endogenous Social Effects: The Reflection Problem." *Review of Economic Studies,* 60(3): 531–542.

Marschak, J., and W. Andrews. 1944. "Random Simultaneous Equations and the Theory of Production." *Econometrica,* 12: 143–205.

Meijl, J. C. M. 1995. *Endogenous Technological Change: The Case of Information Technology.* Maastricht: Maastricht University Press.

Mendershausen, H. 1938. "On the Significance of Professor Douglas' Production Function." *Econometrica,* 6(2): 143–153.

Metcalfe, J. S. 1997. "The Evolutionary Explanation of Total Factor Productivity Growth: Macro Measurement and Micro Process." CRIC Discussion Paper no. 1, June, University of Manchester.

Miller, H. P. 1960. "Annual and Lifetime Income in Relation to Education." *American Economic Review,* 50: 962–986.

Minasian, J. 1962a. "Technical Change and Production Function." *Econometrica,* 30(2): 370–371.

―――― 1962b. "The Economics of Research and Development." In R. R. Nelson, ed., *The Rate and Direction of Inventive Activity,* pp. 93–142. NBER Special Conference vol. 13. Princeton: Princeton University Press.

―――― 1969. "Research and Development, Production Functions, and Rates of Return." *American Economic Review, Papers and Proceedings,* 59(2): 80–85.

Mincer, J. 1958. "Investment on Human Capital and Personal Income Distribution." *Journal of Political Economics,* 66: 281–302.

―――― 1974. *Schooling, Experience, and Earnings.* New York: Columbia University Press for NBER.

―――― 1993. "Human Capital Responses to Technological Change in the Labor Market." In *Studies in Human Capital, Collected Essays of Jacob Mincer,* vol. 1, pp. 345–365. Hants, Eng.: Edward Elgar.

Mohnen, P. 1996. "R&D Externalities and Productivity Growth." *STI Review,* 18: 39–66.

―――― 1997. "Introduction: Input-Output Analysis of Interindustry R&D Spillovers." *Economic Systems Research,* 9(1): 3–8.

Mokyr, J. 1990. *Twenty-Five Centuries of Technological Change: An Historical Survey.* Fundamentals of Pure and Applied Economics, vol. 35. New York: Harwood Academic Publishers.

Mueller, D. 1967. "The Firm Decision Process: An Econometric Investigation." *Quarterly Journal of Economics,* 81(February): 58–87.

Mundlak, Y. 1993. "On the Empirical Aspects of Economic Growth Theory." *American Economic Review*, 83(2): 415–420.

Murphy, K. M., and F. Welch. 1992. "The Structure of Wages." *Quarterly Journal of Economics*, 107: 215–226.

—— 1993. "Industrial Change and the Rising Importance of Skill." In S. Danziger and P. Gottschalk, eds., *Uneven Tides: Rising Inequality in America*, pp. 101–132. New York: Russell Sage Foundation.

Nadiri, M. I. 1993. "Innovations and Technological Spillovers." NBER Working Paper no. 4423. Cambridge, Mass.: National Bureau of Economic Research.

Nadiri, M. I., and S. Kim. 1996. "International R&D Spillovers, Trade, and Productivity in Major OECD Countries." NBER Working Paper no. 5801. Cambridge, Mass.: National Bureau of Economics Research.

Nadiri, M. I., and I. Prucha. 1996."Estimation of the Depreciation Rate of Physical and R&D Capital in the U.S. Total Manufacturing Sector." *Economic Inquiry*, 34(January): 43–56.

Narin, F., K. S. Hamilton, and D. Olivastro. 1997. "The Increasing Linkage between U.S. Technology and Public Science." *Research Policy*, 26(3): 317–330.

National Science Board. 1998. *Science and Engineering Indicators, 1998*. NSF 98–1. Arlington, Va.: National Science Foundation.

National Science Foundation. 1996. *Research and Development in Industry, 1993*. NSF 96–304. Arlington, Va.: National Science Foundation.

—— 1999a. *Research and Development in Industry, 1997*. Arlington, Va.: National Science Foundation.

—— 1999b. *National Patterns of R&D Resources, 1998*, by Steven Payson. Arlington, Va.: National Science Foundation.

Nelson, R. R. 1959. "The Simple Economics of Basic Scientific Research." *Journal of Political Economy*, 67(June): 297–306.

—— ed., 1962a. *The Rate and Direction of Inventive Activity: Economic and Social Factors*. NBER Conference Series no. 13. Princeton: Princeton University Press.

—— 1962b. "The Link between Science and Invention: The Case of the Transistor." In R. R. Nelson, ed., *The Rate and Direction of Inventive Activity*, pp. 549–586. Princeton: Princeton University Press.

—— 1964. "Aggregate Production Functions and Medium-range Growth Projections." *American Economic Review*, 65(5): 575–606.

Nelson, R. R., and E. S. Phelps. 1966. "Investment in Humans, Technological Diffusion, and Economic Growth." *American Economic Review*, 56: 69–75.

Nickell, S., and D. Nicolitsas. 1996. "Does Innovation Encourage Investment in Fixed Capital." Unpublished paper, Institute of Economics and Statistics, Oxford University, September.

Nordhaus, W. 1972. "The Recent Productivity Slowdown." *Brookings Papers on Economic Activity*, 3: 493–545.

OECD. 1996. *Technology and Industrial Performance.* Paris: OECD.

Office of Technology Assessment. 1986. *Research Funding as an Investment: Can We Measure the Returns?* Technical Memorandum. Washington, D.C.: U.S. Congress.

Olley, S., and A. Pakes. 1996. "The Dynamics of Productivity in the Telecommunications Equipment Industry." *Econometrica*, 64(6): 1263–1297.

Oniki, H. 1968. "A Theoretical Study on the Demand for Education." Ph.D. diss., Stanford University.

Pakes, A. 1986. "Patents as Options: Some Estimates of the Value of Holding European Patent Stocks." *Econometrica*, 54(4): 755–784.

Pakes, A., and Z. Griliches. 1984. "Estimating Distributed Lags in Short Panels with an Application to the Specification of Depreciation Patterns and Capital Stock Constructs." *Review of Economic Studies*, 51(2): 243–262.

Pakes, A., and M. Schankerman. 1984. "The Rate of Obsolescence of Patents, Research Gestation Lags, and the Private Rate of Return to Research Resources." In Z. Griliches, ed., *R&D, Patents, and Productivity*, pp. 73–88. Chicago: University of Chicago Press.

Parente, S., and E. Prescott. 1994. "Barriers to Technology Adoption and Development." *Journal of Political Economy*, 102(2): 298–321.

Park, W. G. 1995. "International R&D Spillovers and OECD Economic Growth." *Economic Inquiry*, 33: 571–591.

Romer, P. M. 1990a. "Endogenous Technological Change." *Journal of Political Economy*, 98(5): S71–S102.

Rosen, S. 1973. "Income Generating Functions and Capital Accumulation." Harvard Institute of Economic Research Discussion Paper no. 306, Harvard University.

Rosenberg, N. 1996. "Uncertainty and Technical Change." In J. Fuhrer and J. S. Little, eds., *Technology and Growth*, pp. 91–110 (with discussions by J. Mokyr, pp. 111–118, and L. Soete, pp. 119–125). Boston: Federal Reserve Bank.

Ruttan, V. W. 1954. *Technological Progress in the Meat Packing Industry, 1919–47.* Washington, D.C.: U.S. Department of Agriculture.

———— 1956. "The Contribution of Technological Progress to Farm Output, 1950–75." *Review of Economics and Statistics*, 38(1): 61–69.

Rymes, T. K. 1971. *On Concepts of Capital and Technical Change.* Cambridge: Cambridge University Press.

Sakurai, N., G. Papaconstantinou, and E. Ioannidis. 1995. "The Impact of R&D and Technology Diffusion on Productivity Growth: Evidence for Ten OECD Countries in the 1970s and 1980s." Manuscript, OECD, Paris.

Schankerman, M. 1981. "The Effects of Double-Counting and Expensing on the Measured Returns to R&D." *Review of Economics and Statistics,* 63(3): 454–458.

Schankerman, M., and A. Pakes. 1986. "Estimates of the Value of Patent Rights in European Countries during the Post-1950 Period." *Economic Journal,* 96(384): 1052–1076.

Scherer, F. M. 1965. "Corporate Inventive Output, Profits, and Growth." *Journal of Political Economy,* 73: 290–297.

——— 1982. "Interindustry Technology Flows and Productivity Growth." *Review of Economics and Statistics,* 64(4): 627–634.

——— 1984. "Using Linked Patent and R&D Data to Measure Interindustry Technology Flows." In Z. Griliches, ed., *R&D, Patents, and Productivity,* pp. 417–461. Chicago: University of Chicago Press.

Schmookler, J. 1951. "Invention and Economic Development." Ph.D. diss., University of Pennsylvania, Philadelphia.

——— 1952. "The Changing Efficiency of the American Economy, 1869–1938." *Review of Economics and Statistics,* 34(3): 214–231.

——— 1954. "The Level of Inventive Activity." *Review of Economics and Statistics,* 36(May): 183–190.

Schultz, T. W. 1953. *The Economic Organization of Agriculture.* New York: McGraw-Hill.

——— 1956. "Reflections on Agricultural Production, Output, and Supply." *Journal of Farm Economics,* 38(3): 748–762.

——— 1960. "Capital Formation by Education." *Journal of Political Economy,* 68: 571–583.

——— 1990. *Restoring Economic Equilibrium.* London: Blackwell.

Sheshinski, E. 1968. "On the Individual's Lifetime Allocation between Education and Work." *Metroeconomica,* 20: 42–49.

Singer, C., ed. 1954–1984. *A History of Technology,* 8 vols. Oxford: Clarendon Press.

Smith, V. E. 1940. "An Application and Critique of Certain Methods for the Determination of a Statistical Production Function for the Canadian Automobile Industry, 1917–1930." Ph.D. diss., Northwestern University.

Solow, R. M. 1956. "A Contribution to the Theory of Economic Growth." *Quarterly Journal of Economics*, 70(February): 65–94.

———— 1957. "Technical Change and the Aggregate Production Function." *Review of Economics and Statistics*, 39(3): 312–320.

———— 1960. "Investment and Technical Progress." In K. J. Arrow et al., eds., *Mathematical Methods of the Social Sciences*. Stanford: Stanford University Press.

———— 1997. "How Did Economics Get That Way and What Way Did It Get?" *Daedalus*, 126(1): 39–58.

Spence, M. 1974. *Market Signaling*. Cambridge, Mass.: Harvard University Press.

Science Policy Research Unit (SPRU). 1996. *The Relationship between Publicly Funded Basic Research and Economic Performance*. Report for HM Treasury, University of Sussex.

Srinivasan, S. 1996. "Estimation of Own R&D, R&D Spillovers, and Exogenous Technical Change Effects in Some U.S. High-Technology Industries." DP9607, Department of Economics, University of Southampton (based on University of Maryland thesis).

Stephan, P. 1996. "An Essay on the Economics of Science." *Journal of Economic Literature*, 34: 1199–1235.

Stigler, G. 1947. *Trends in Output and Employment*. New York: National Bureau of Economic Research.

Summers, R., and A. Heston. 1991. "The Penn World Table (Mark 5): An Expanded Set of International Comparisons, 1950–1988." *Quarterly Journal of Economics*, 106: 327–368.

Sveikauskas, L. 1989. *The Impact of R&D on Productivity Growth*. BLS Bulletin no. 2331. Washington, D.C.: Government Printing Office.

———— 1995. "The Indirect Effect of R&D." Unpublished paper, Bureau of Labor Statistics, Washington, D.C.

Terleckyj, N. 1958. "Factors Underlying Productivity: Some Empirical Observations." *Journal of the American Statistical Association*, 53(June): 593.

———— 1974. *Effects of R&D on the Productivity Growth of Industries: An Exploratory Study*. Washington, D.C.: National Planning Association.

Tinbergen, J. 1941. *Econometrie*. Gorinchem, Netherlands: J. Noorduijn en zoon n.v.

———— 1942. "Zur Theorie der Langfirstigen Wirtschaftsentwicklung." *Weltwirtschafliches Archiv* (Amesterdam), 1: 511–549. Reprinted in English translation in J. Tinbergen, *Selected Papers* (Amsterdam: North-Holland, 1959).

Tintner, G. 1943. *Econometrics*. New York: Wiley, 1952.

———— 1944. "A Note on the Derivation of Production Functions from Farm Records." *Econometrica*, 12(1): 26–34.

———— 1946. "Some Applications of Multivariate Analysis to Economic Data." *Journal of the American Statistical Association*, 41(December): 472–500.

U.S. Department of Agriculture. 1991. *Agricultural Statistics, 1991*. Washington, D.C.: U.S.Department of Agriculture.

Usher, A. P. 1954. *A History of Mechanical Inventions*. Cambridge, Mass.: Harvard University Press.

Valvanis-Vail, S. 1955. "An Econometric Model of Growth, USA, 1869–1953." *American Economic Review*, 45 (Supp.): 208–221.

van Pottelsberghe, B. 1996. "Inter-Industry Technological Spillovers and the Rate for Return to R&D." Discussion Paper 96-DOF 23, Ministry of International Trade and Industry (MITI), Tokyo, April.

Weiss, Y. 1986. "The Determination of Life Cycle Earnings: A Survey." In O. Ashenfelter and R. Layard, eds., *Handbook of Labor Economics*, pp. 603–640. Amsterdam: North-Holland.

Welch, F. 1970. "Education in Production." *Journal of Political Economy*, 78: 35–59.

Willis, R. J. 1986. "Wage Determinants: A Survey and Reinterpretation of Human Capital Earnings Functions." In O. Ashenfelter and R. Layard, eds., *Handbook of Labor Economics*, pp. 525–602. Amsterdam: North-Holland.

Wolpin, K. 1977. "Education and Screening." *American Economic Review*, 67: 949–958.

Vaizey, J., et al. 1964. *The Residual Factor and Economic Growth*. Paris: OECD.

CREDITS

An earlier version of Chapter 1 appeared as "The Discovery of the Residual: A Historical Note" in the *Journal of Economic Literature*, 34 (1996): 1324–1330. An earlier version of Chapter 3 appeared as "Education, Human Capital, and Growth: A Personal Perspective" in the *Journal of Labor Economics*, 15(1, pt. 2): S330–S344. An earlier version of Chapter 4 appeared as "R&D and Productivity: The Unfinished Business" in my book *R&D and Productivity: The Econometric Evidence* (Chicago: University of Chicago Press, 1998; © 1998 by The University of Chicago). Figure 2.1 is reproduced with the permission of Kluwer Academic Publishers from Robert J. Gordon, "Current Productivity Puzzles from a Long-term Perspective," in B. van Art, S. Kuipers, and G. Kuper, eds., *Productivity, Technology, and Economic Growth* (Dordrecht: Kluwer Academic Publishers, 2000).

INDEX